'The Pit Station can now clear so *Thrust* the car began to roll very slowly, then got faster and faster until it was zooming through the measured mile completely silent . . .'

JACK NOBLE: *Richard Noble's son*
From the scene of the record-breaking attempt in
Nevada
October 1997

This book is dedicated to the ThrustSSC team

THE STORY OF *ThrustSSC*
A CORGI BOOK : 0 552 546410

First publication in Great Britain

PRINTING HISTORY
Corgi edition published 1998

With acknowledgements and thanks to
Dave Morris, Ron Ayers and Glynne Bowsher
for the preparation of the manuscript

Set in 12pt Palatino
by Phoenix Typesetting, Ilkley, West Yorkshire

Corgi Books are published by Transworld Publishers Ltd,
61–63 Uxbridge Road, Ealing, London W5 5SA,
in Australia by Transworld Publishers (Australia) Pty. Ltd,
15–25 Helles Avenue, Moorebank, NSW 2170,
and in New Zealand by Transworld Publishers (NZ) Ltd,
3 William Pickering Drive, Albany, Auckland.

Made and printed in Great Britain by
Cox & Wyman Ltd, Reading, Berkshire.

THE STORY OF

THRUST SSC

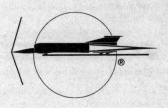

The world's

first supersonic

World Land

Speed Record

CORGI BOOKS

For more information on *ThrustSSC*,
check out the *ThrustSSC* website on:

http://thrustssc.digital.co.uk

Acknowledgements

With thanks to the following for their permission to reproduce the
following photographs and diagrams:

Castrol: p5 (engines), p6 (stationary car), p8 (SSC team)
Alain Ernoult/Paris Match: p5 (Andy Green in front of car),
p6 (three photos), p8 (Jack)
Richard Meredith-Hardy: p7

The remaining pictures are taken from the private collections of the
Authors. Every effort has been made to trace the copyright owners, but
anyone who feels his or her copyright has been infringed is invited to
contact the Authors c/o the Publishers.

PROLOGUE

On a chilly morning in October 1997, Richard Noble drove out into the Nevada desert. To his right, the first glimmer of sunrise was visible as an orange glow behind the mountains which border the Black Rock desert. In the crisp air, Richard could see steam rising from the hot springs along the edge of the road.

All the signs were that it was to be just another day. But Richard knew differently. Today was the day he'd been working towards for half his life.

Today, if everything went well, history would be made. For the first time, Man would achieve the very first supersonic land speed record . . .

Part I

THE THRUST PROJECT

ONE

Richard Noble's dream of breaking the land speed record had begun when he was only six years old. His father had taken him for a drive and they saw a monster on Loch Ness.

It wasn't the scaly *Jurassic Park* kind of monster. It was a 40-foot jet-powered hydroplane, silver trimmed with goldfish red, that dwarfed all the other boats on the loch.

His father stopped the car and they walked down for a closer look. 'It's *Crusader*,' someone said. 'The boat that's going to break the water speed record.'

The boat was a beauty. Its long sleek shape and the torpedo-shaped sponsons outrigged at the back made it look as though it would run on skis. But it wasn't the boat itself that inspired Richard. It was the element of speed, the idea of a craft fitted with an aeroplane engine travelling faster than any surface-bound vehicle had ever travelled before.

He didn't know it then, but that idea would eventually make him the fastest man in the world.

Challengers have been competing for the land speed record for a hundred years. In 1898 a Frenchman, Count Gaston de Chasseloup Laubat, climbed into the very first land-speed record car and drove at a little under forty miles per hour. For those days, that was a record!

Others soon improved on that first speed. Within six years the record had gone through the 100 m.p.h. mark. Sir Malcolm Campbell set records throughout the 1920s and 1930s, culminating in a speed of 301 m.p.h. set in September 1935. By the time Richard was ten, the World Land Speed Record stood at 394 m.p.h. to John Cobb.

In those days, the rules still only catered for cars that transmitted their power through the wheels (like a normal car). It wasn't until the 1960s that American contenders such as Dr Nathan Ostich, Craig Breedlove, Tom Green and Art Arfons brought in the era of turbo-jet powered cars, which were literally blown along by their own exhaust gases. These cars had phenomenal power and no need for a complex, heavy and power-absorbing transmission, so they were able to accelerate a lot faster and the land speed record went from 400 m.p.h to 600 m.p.h. in less than two years.

JET PROPULSION

Imagine standing on roller skates and throwing a ball. The reaction would mean that while the ball flew off quickly in one direction, you'd move (more slowly) in the opposite direction. This is Newton's third law: for every action there's an equal and opposite reaction.

A jet engine works by sucking air into an air compressor, compressing it, and then passing it into a combustion chamber where fuel is burned to rapidly heat up and expand the air. The exhaust gases then leave the combustion chamber at a much higher velocity than the air enters, and after powering a turbine which drives the compressor, pass out of the back of the engine as jet thrust.

As the gases race out of the jet exhaust, so the reaction propels the jet engine forwards.

As a child, Richard started collecting anything he could find on speed attempts, with the land-speed record uppermost in his thoughts. He would sketch record cars in his school exercise books and when he was older, he would scour scrapyards, trying to find old spark plugs that were just the right shape for the cardboard jet-engine mock-up he had built. He read a book called *Rocket Propulsion* by Eric Burgess over and over again (he still has it). Almost without realizing, Richard became obsessed with the land-speed record.

When Richard left school, he tried a variety of different careers and also went on an incredible overland expedition in Africa, where he met Sally, who was later to become his wife. But the idea of the land-speed record was always there in the background and by the time Richard was almost twenty-eight, its call had become irresistible. He decided that he wasn't going to waste any more time – he was going to build and drive the fastest car in the world.

Richard had no engineering skills and no money, so the first steps were obvious if a little daunting. He had to learn how to build a jet car, and he somehow had to find all the parts for next to nothing. Certainly those were simple stages – but they wouldn't prove all that easy!

He decided to start by building a first car, which he would call *Thrust1*. The name 'Thrust' seemed ideal for the project, since the kind of vehicle Richard was planning to build was powered by a jet engine. The idea was to learn the ropes by building *Thrust1*. Later, Richard planned to progress to *Thrust2*, which he envisaged as a demonstration car that he could use to raise sponsorship for the final and most ambitious vehicle: *Thrust3*.

It was *Thrust3* in which, Richard hoped, he could become the world land speed champion.

TWO

The first thing was to decide what sort of car *Thrust1* was going to be. Richard chose a straightforward ladder-type chassis frame with a very simple jet engine mounted on it. It needed to be a simple engine because Richard would have to install it and get it running by himself. He chose to use a jet engine rather than a rocket for a number of different reasons, one of which was that second-hand jet engines were cheaper and easier to find, since the military often sell them off when they are no longer needed.

The simplest engine available at the time was the Rolls-Royce Derwent. The best model, the Mark IX, was all but impossible to get hold of. But the RAF were selling off a lot of their Mark

VIIIs which had been used as snowblowers to clear runways.

Richard began his search at the RAF Museum in Hendon, where he was able to get an instruction manual on the Derwent engine. Studying that gave him a good grasp of the Derwent's design and layout, but of course he still needed to lay his hands on one. A family friend told him that a scrapyard in Portsmouth had just acquired thirty Derwents from the RAF.

Richard took the next train to Portsmouth and was amazed. All these jet engines were just lying around on the ground. He was in his element. He spent the afternoon checking them out. There was one in particular that was ideal. It had only a few hundred hours running time on it, which meant that it had plenty of service life left. This was a real stroke of luck, because most jet engines are scrapped only when they've reached the end of their useful life. And even better, with this engine went one of the only good jet pipes to be had anywhere in Britain.

Richard said to the scrap dealer, 'I've got to have this one.'

The scrap dealer started to tell him the price.

Richard interrupted: 'I can only give you

two hundred pounds.'

The scrap dealer tried haggling, but Richard was hard to resist. Eventually the dealer threw up his hands. 'All right, two hundred pounds it is. But there's one thing: the French government are sending someone to look at these engines the day after tomorrow. The French often buy Derwents off me, in fact they're my best customers. I can't let them see this engine because they'll want it, and you don't refuse your best customer! So if you want it, you'll have to take it away before they arrive.'

Now that he'd found his engine, Richard wasn't going to let it go. He managed to borrow a truck in London, drove down the next day, and hoisted the Derwent onto the back. The French government never knew what a bargain they'd missed.

For a chassis, Richard obtained a ladder chassis which had been a development unit at the GKN factory in Telford. With a combination of persuasion and dogged persistence, Richard managed to scrape together everything he needed to build *Thrust1*: a fuel pump from RAF Kemble; a hot end from RAF Stafford; and a starter panel – which was where he very nearly met his match.

15

The starter panel had lots of relays and electrically wound clocks. Richard only had the one panel, so there was no room for trial-and-error learning. He hardly knew where to start. He went right through the manual, but the diagrams were no help. Wiring up the panel looked like being a nightmare – and Richard was no electrician.

He sought out the designer of the starter panel, a splendid old character who was delighted that something he'd designed back in the 1940s should still have a use thirty years later. With his help, Richard was able to start wiring it all up.

Now that he had started to build the car, one of the biggest design considerations he had to resolve was how to avoid the car's nose lifting at high speeds.

LIFT

As a vehicle moves, it cuts through the air, forcing the air to flow round it. The different speeds at which the air flows over, under and around the vehicle are very important because they create areas of low and high pressure around the body of the vehicle.

This is the same principle that makes an aeroplane's wing work. If the wing moves through the air at the correct angle, its shape makes the air flow faster above the wing than below. This difference in the speed of the airflow creates lower pressure above the wing than below, which gives the wing lift and makes it possible for the aeroplane to fly.

These forces are also at work on earth-bound vehicles and are an important factor for the designer who, amongst other things, has to be certain that the differences in pressure will keep the vehicle on the ground – that it will not 'fly'. The angle at which the nose of the vehicle attacks the air is crucial for getting these pressures right. Slightly too much of a 'nose-up' angle will result in up-forces under the vehicle, while too much of a 'nose-down' angle could create significant down-forces above the vehicle. When the vehicle is moving slowly, the differences of pressure are there but not very great. The faster the vehicle goes, the larger these forces become and when it is moving at very high speeds, at some point the comforting assumption that the vehicle will stay on the ground is going to be lost. The car could take off and crash at horribly high speeds, risking the life of the driver.

The most vivid and tragic example of the dangers involved was the horrific accident in which Donald Campbell lost his life. His jet-powered boat, *Bluebird*, flipped over on Coniston Water at more than 300 m.p.h. during his last record attempt in 1967.

Richard still had a full-time job at this point – and still had no money – so he gradually put the car together by working in his spare time and at weekends. Slowly, *Thrust1* began to take shape. But it wasn't much to look at. It had big nose wings at the front to give negative lift at high speed. 'It was like a go-kart on steroids,' was Richard's own impression.

Then came the time to give the car its first test run. Richard tracked down the UK's last specialist on the Derwent Mark VIII, Sergeant Jim Matthews at RAF St Athan in South Wales. At first Jim was very sceptical about the chances of the thing working, but after a few adjustments he decided it would be all right and they were ready to give the engine its first static test.

They tethered *Thrust1* down and Jim said 'Right, Richard, off you go!'

Richard had to confess to feeling a little nervous. If he opened the high-pressure fuel cock incorrectly, it could set off resonance which might damage the engine and, also, nearby buildings.

He looked at Jim. 'Well, hang on,' he said, 'I've never done this before. I don't want to wreck it. Would you...?'

Jim shook his head. 'No, you built the damned thing, you're going to be the one sitting in it when we fire it up!'

Tentatively Richard fired the engine up. There was a low droning sound as the turbine started up, then the *whoosh* of the torch ignitors lighting up the fuel in the combustion chambers. The sound was like solid waves of vibration in the air. Rapidly it built in pitch until that familiar whine known to every aircraft passenger filled the airfield.

It was like having a tiger tethered in a cage. He couldn't wait to untether it, to feel that force driving him down the runway outside.

Later that afternoon, that was exactly what he did. For its first outing, the plan was to run *Thrust1* at no more than 70 or 80 m.p.h. It was just a shakedown run to make sure that everything worked properly.

Richard sat in the open cockpit watching the revs rising. He eased the high-pressure fuel cock open, just as he had done that morning in the hangar. Suddenly there was a *whoomph* as the engine lit up. He released the brakes and the car was away.

For Richard it was the moment he had worked for. The first stage of a project that less than ten years later would earn him the world land speed record.

But there was no time then to relax. He still had a lot of work in front of him. The next step was to find a good long runway where he could give *Thrust1* full throttle.

Again the location chosen was an RAF base, this time RAF Fairford in Gloucester. There was only one possible snag: Fairford was an operational base, meaning that aircraft also used the runway, although not all the time. Richard was able to get a special licence to take *Thrust1* out when the runway wasn't in use.

'It was the morning of 7 March 1977,' remembers Richard. 'The weather was dreadful, and I'd been up half the night making last-minute adjustments. Anyway, we got *Thrust1* lit up and did one westerly run at about 180 m.p.h., despite a severe crosswind. That was fantastic. I got a real sense of high velocity, especially with the open cockpit and the wind rasping past my head.

'I then turned the car around for another go. This time I didn't start gently. I held as much thrust as possible against the brakes, then released them and did a dragster start up to 140 m.p.h. My plan was then to let the car coast the remainder of the 3000-metre runway.'

It went well at first, but at around 140 m.p.h. he suddenly lost control of *Thrust1*. There was no warning. It just went. It was a fearsome feeling. It wasn't an ordinary car and he had no motor-racing experience, and suddenly there was a situation where the car just went sideways and then crashed. It rolled over and over and finally came to a rest upside down after a triple airborne roll.

'Richard went charging up the runway and was almost out of sight when we saw something happen. I could see a billowing white cloud of what I thought at the time was smoke. When the fire engine sped off, I panicked.

'However, even before we got to the scene of the accident I could see it wasn't as bad as all that. Richard had struggled out of the wreck and was walking about, so I knew he was OK.

'Later one of the firemen said to me, "You shouldn't have worried, Mrs Noble. We knew it wasn't anything serious. If it had been black smoke then we would have hurried, because that means fire. But all you saw was vapour."'

– SALLY NOBLE, *Richard's wife*

The large diameter of the Derwent engine may have saved Richard's life. It had acted like a giant rollover hoop, taking all the impact of the crash. Richard was just left dangling in his seatbelts.

Examining the wreck later, they discovered that a rear wheel bearing had seized up, throwing the car out of control. That single thing had resulted in *Thrust1* being reduced to a pile of scrap.

But Richard didn't see it as a failure – not even as a setback. After all, no-one had been hurt and he'd done what he set out to do. The mechanical fault with the wheel bearing was a valuable lesson for the future. The thing now was to get straight on with *Thrust2*.

On the way back home to London, he stopped off at a scrapyard and sold the wreck of *Thrust1* for £175. He was concerned at the dreamy look in the dealer's eyes when he looked at the car. He seemed to have some notion of getting it running again. Since it had come within a whisker of killing Richard, that would not be a good idea, so he made sure to remove enough components so that there was no way *Thrust1* would ever move under its own power again.

THREE

What would the new car look like? *Thrust1* had served as an introduction for the project, but *Thrust2* had to be the real thing. For a start, it would have to have a professional designer if Richard was to have a hope of coming close to the land speed record. The design would be more complex than for *Thrust1*, and called for more expertise than Richard himself had.

But until he could find an expert, Richard began work on some preliminary sketches. He could at least get the basic layout of the design worked out and look for an engine.

In the 1960s, Art Arfons' *Green Monster* jet car had set the land speed record three times in a series of gripping duels with Arfons' rival Craig Breedlove. Breedlove's three-wheeler, *Spirit of America*, had crashed into a brine lake when he lost his parachutes at well over 500 m.p.h., and for the next car he had decided on a four-wheeler. This was a long slender-shaped car with the driver sitting ahead of the engine. It was the same layout that Richard had used – somewhat less elegantly – with *Thrust1*.

For *Thrust2*, Richard decided to use the *Green Monster* layout (see p83). This did away with the need for a complicated air intake because the engine was simply mounted head-on with the driver sitting alongside it, midway down its length. It was safer because it was shorter and thus allowed for a more robust structure. And the driver would be safer sitting alongside the engine. This design also had the advantage of having room for a second seat on the other side of the engine.

Since Richard had originally intended that *Thrust2* should be a vehicle that he could show off to raise media interest and sponsorship, including a passenger seat would make it possible to take potential sponsors for a spin. Just as long as it didn't give them a heart attack, the ride might be a good way to encourage them to sponsor the *Thrust* project. Not that he had any sponsors yet.

He had a lucky break when he was looking

for an engine for the car. He was able to borrow the money to buy a Rolls-Royce Avon 210 turbojet, which had come from a Lightning fighter plane when it was taken out of service. He also managed to find a number of other useful Lightning components in a scrapyard.

Richard's sketches of what he thought *Thrust2* might look like had become quite detailed by now. It was a blunt racer with a large shark-fin tail, a huge aerofoil at the front, and four front wheels. But having got that far, he threw down his pencil. There was no way he had the skills needed to design a car that had a realistic hope of breaking the record.

It was time to find a real designer.

How do you go about finding someone to design a jet-powered car? It looked a tricky problem at first, but very often the best way to solve a problem is the most direct. Richard simply put out a press release: *Wanted: 650 m.p.h. car designer*. The press release was run in a large number of major papers, including the *Daily Telegraph*.

As luck would have it, Richard had to go abroad on business for six weeks. When he got back there was a stack of replies to his press release. In particular there had been urgent calls from a man named John Ackroyd.

After meeting 'Ackers', as he soon got to be known, Richard was impressed but he wanted a second opinion. He called Ken Norris, who had designed the *Bluebird K7* hydroplane in which Donald Campbell had taken the water speed record in the 1960s, to ask if he would interview Ackers too.

'I think he's good, but will you see him?' asked Richard.

'I already have. He's been here all morning!' replied Norris.

It was confirmation of Ackers' enthusiasm, and Richard knew he had found his designer.

Ackers got plenty of practical and invaluable advice from Ken Norris, which included the aerodynamics.

Ackers concentrated on refining *Thrust2*'s design while Richard set about raising money for the project.

By March 1978 they were ready to start building the car. Ackers' new design featured a big tubular spaceframe with the Avon jet mounted between the driver and passenger seats. Since Ackers came from the Isle of Wight and knew many highly skilled and experienced engineers who lived locally, it was decided to base the operation down there. But if they began with any dream of a huge, well-fitted workshop, those dreams were soon dashed. The project had just enough money to rent a derelict house. Ackers set up his drawing-board in the kitchen and worked there for ten hard months. There was certainly no modern equipment. The only phone was a callbox nearby, the nearest photocopier was a six-mile ride away, and to get drawings printed he had to take a fourteen-mile hike to East Cowes. If it hadn't been for love of the project he would certainly have given up.

While Ackers and his team were working on building the car, Richard had to spend every spare moment making sure the cash was coming in. The project was growing week by week, and every time Richard raised a bit more sponsorship money it was gone on whatever the team needed to make or buy next.

A lucky break came when Ackers needed to make the driver's seat. He wanted to get a good feel for the size of the cockpit. The seat had to be moulded around Richard, who had the bright idea of inviting the *Tomorrow's World* programme from the BBC to film the process. When it was shown on TV, it brought in the project's main sponsor, a company called Initial Services. Together with other financial sponsors, the money they put in gave just enough leeway for the project to continue until the first test runs. It would be make or break for the *Thrust* project.

Places like RAF Fairford, where *Thrust1* had been run, were operational military bases where the RAF probably didn't object to lending their runway for a few hours at a weekend, but the test runs for *Thrust2* would take a whole week or more. The team would need to do a run, assess the data, make adjustments, try another run – and so on. No matter how accommodating the RAF had been before, you couldn't expect them to have the patience for that.

An alternative was to use a dragstrip such as Santa Pod, near Bedford, but the drawback there was lack of space. What was needed was a long stretch where the car could just run on if the brakes failed.

Finally, Richard settled on Normandy Barracks, Leconfield, just north of Humberside. It had formerly been an active airbase but was now an army training centre. It had a long stretch of runway that was used for training army truck drivers and seemed perfect for *Thrust2*.

Only, once he got there, he started to have doubts about himself.

The problem was the first few runs. The whole team pitched in to help, and naturally they expected great things. There was this powerful machine – at this stage still an unclad chassis with a Rolls-Royce jet mounted on it – and everyone thought they'd see something spectacular straight away.

Instead, Richard trundled off at a speed that he thought was about 70 m.p.h. It turned out to be only 50 m.p.h.

'With jet-powered cars you have to start out carefully,' protested Richard. Even he had to admit that he was disappointed with the speeds he was getting, though. With each run he edged up towards 200 m.p.h., but couldn't quite seem to get there. He was also very cautious with the afterburner.

THE AFTERBURNER

Jet engines get an extra boost in power by using an afterburner. The afterburner is bolted to the back of the engine and the jet exhaust passes through it. Neat fuel is injected into the exhaust, burning up the remaining oxygen, a process known as reheat, causing further expansion and increase in exhaust velocity and hence thrust.

The afterburner creates a huge roaring flame and can increase the engine power by 50% or more. In fighter aircraft it is usually used for take off and for rapid acceleration in combat – but only in short bursts as it consumes huge quantities of fuel.

Part of the trouble Richard was having was that Leconfield wasn't as ideal a track as it had first seemed. For one thing, half way down the runway was a major intersection with traffic lights. For some reason it was impossible to switch the lights off, so Richard was faced with a serious distraction every time he ran the car. With the best will in the world, it is hard to overcome the psychological block of racing towards a set of red lights at close to 200 m.p.h.

As if that wasn't bad enough, there was a large hump half way down the runway – as he drove up the hump, he was unable to see what was on the other side. Richard was uncomfortable because he felt as if he was driving blind. What if he got over the hump to find that someone had wandered onto the runway dead in front of him? He could tell himself time and again that every safety precaution had been taken, that it couldn't happen. But all the same it meant that he couldn't quite bring himself to pull out all the stops.

It was a worrying thought. Designs can be refined, components replaced. It's not so easy to fix a fault that lies in yourself.

'We managed to edge up to a shade under a hundred and ninety, but I was pretty timid with the afterburner and frankly I was a bit scared of the thing. I really needed to get to grips with it. It was the psychology of it all, the hump and traffic lights and all the rest of it. I just didn't seem to get my act together.'

— RICHARD NOBLE

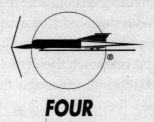

FOUR

On the way back to the Isle of Wight, everyone was a bit disheartened. They'd expected more. Richard tried to get them to concentrate on the positive aspects of the trip. The purpose of going to Leconfield had been to get away from the outside world and pressure from the media, so that they could focus on learning about the car. And they had learned a great deal.

'We'll get there,' Richard assured them. 'Just stick with it.'

It was something he himself desperately wanted to believe. What if, after all his hard work, he wasn't cut out to be a champion? He was hardly looking forward to the next thing on their schedule, a public exhibition at HMS *Daedalus* at Lee-on-Solent (a naval shore-base). At daybreak it was pouring with rain, but later it let up and Richard did a 180 m.p.h. demonstration run for the press towards noon.

After lunch he was due to run again. By this time the sun had come out and the temperature had risen. As he walked to the car, Richard felt different somehow.

He cracked off down the runway. The speed went to 180, 190 . . . through the 200 m.p.h. mark. And then everything just clicked. Richard's focus was absolute. There were no distractions now. He was accelerating in the four-tonne car, using maximum afterburner and revelling in the sheer power of the vehicle they had built.

Everything had come together, just as he had said. Richard's faith – in the rest of the team and in himself – had been vindicated.

From this point on, everything seemed to come together really well. After a summer spent travelling around air shows throughout Great Britain, Richard felt it was time to move on to the next stage – to attack the British land speed record. The record currently stood at 191.64 m.p.h., the holder being Robert Horne in a Ferrari 512M racing sportscar, and Richard and the rest of the team felt confident that *Thrust2* was ready for the challenge.

'We had quite a difficult time when we went to Greenham to attempt the British Land Speed Record, because we were pushing the car absolutely to its limits on the short runway. I was braking very hard rom more than 250 m.p.h., and finishing up just 4 metres from the end of the runway. It was really stretching the car, and it was really stretching me. But then it all came together'

— RICHARD NOBLE

Over the weekend of 24 and 25 September, 1980, Richard claimed six new British records, the most satisfying being the British *Flying Mile* at a speed of 248.87 m.p.h. Now the team had really established themselves. They no longer lacked any credibility. They had done a good job and had proved their ability and commitment.

And there was even better news to come. Ackers had taken a twentieth-scale aluminium model of *Thrust2* to British Aerospace in Weybridge to test in their transonic wind tunnel.

THE WIND TUNNEL

Building a full-size aeroplane is a costly business, and the last thing you would want is to spend all that money and effort only to find that the plane doesn't fly safely.

Fortunately there is an alternative. By blowing air over a scale model in a wind tunnel, the designers can measure very accurately the forces which can be scaled-up to show what would happen to the full-sized aeroplane as it travels at different speeds and under a variety of conditions.

The same principles can be applied to testing racing car designs.

Ackers' hopes for *Thrust2* were that it would be able to reach at least 630 m.p.h. It would need to be impressively fast if it was to be successful at attracting more sponsorship. The wind tunnel test results would let him know for sure.

When the technicians at British Aerospace saw his model they were not complimentary. Their first impression was that the blocky shape would result in severe drag. 'It looks more like a brick on wheels than a car!' said one. All the same, they put it in the wind tunnel.

Ackers went away and waited for the results. That evening he got a call from the head of the testing team.

'Where did you come up with this shape of yours?' he was asked.

'Why?' replied Ackers.

'Well, we can't quite believe it, but the tests show you're on to a winner. *Thrust2* has a potential maximum speed in excess of 650 m.p.h.!'

With that one call, everything changed. Before they had only expected to use *Thrust2* as a demonstration vehicle, not as a serious contender to the land speed record. But the speed set by the reigning world champion, Gary Gabelich, was 622.407 m.p.h. – and the British Aerospace people were saying that *Thrust2* could beat that by a comfortable margin.

Now the next step was clear: they had to make an attempt on the World Land Speed Record with *Thrust2*.

FIVE

At that time, in the early 1980s, the only place to go if you wanted a crack at the land speed record was Bonneville salt flats, in the United States.

Taking *Thrust2* to Bonneville was a bold step, but it was critical for the project to earn credibility. If Richard was going to break the land speed record, he wanted to be sure that the event was properly supervised and witnessed by accredited USAC (United States Auto Club) timekeepers. There needed to be no doubt in anyone's mind.

Somehow they scraped the money together to take the car out to America – some £100,000 in all – mainly thanks to Initial Services and some other big sponsors. Richard was glad to put all the fund-raising and management out of his mind. All he wanted now was to concentrate on driving the car.

BONNEVILLE SALT FLATS

Designing and building a land speed record car is only half of the project – running it and finding somewhere to run it is just as important. The World Land Speed record started off in 1898 on the French roads but soon it was realized that more space and a safer track were needed. The record challengers then transferred to beaches – in particular Pendine in South Wales and Daytona in Florida. But as the speeds approached 300 m.p h. it was quite clear that if the sport was to survive then a better surface and a wider track was needed. An American, Ab Jenkins, was the first to drive on the Bonneville salt flats in the state of Utah, USA.

Bonneville is a vast dried-up lake bed with a very hard salt surface. Most of the year it is flooded – but in September and October the hot sun dries the surface hard enough to race on. Then in late October the winter rains come and the salt flats flood for another year.

Bonneville became the most famous site for the Land Speed Record because of the tremendous grip the salt gave for race car tyres and also because it was very safe: there was plenty of space for a runaway car to lose speed and, if there was an accident, the huge energy in the car would be lost in a long slide on the hard salt with nothing to hit.

For running on the salt flats, *Thrust2* had been fitted with solid aluminium wheels since the jet fighter tyres they had been using so far would not have been able to withstand the huge centrifugal forces involved at record speeds. And they had upgraded the engine to a Rolls-Royce Avon 302, which had been expensive and difficult to fit, but which gave a massive 75,000 newtons of thrust.

'Don't use the reheat,' Ackers advised as he briefed Richard on the detailed run profile. 'Get a feel for how the car handles at slow speed first.'

Richard was filled with excitement. This was the moment he had often anticipated – as a distant dream since he was six, and for the last few years as a definite goal. Now the moment had arrived. He fired the engine up and tried for a steady 100 m.p.h. run.

It was a shambles. He reached 80 m.p.h. and the car slithered off course. The steering felt dead, and at slow speeds, the whole car seemed to want to slide sideways. Richard described it as 'like riding a bicycle with no tyres across a frozen pond'.

With perseverance he got his speed up to 175 m.p.h. Not nearly good enough – not even as fast as those first runs at Leconfield. This time the problem wasn't in his mind, though. It was the car itself. As the speeds advanced, the car became increasingly unstable and would suddenly turn right at 275 m.p.h., running right off the course and two miles into the salt flats. It was lucky they were out in the middle of nowhere – *Thrust2* could safely run miles across the salt flats in any direction it liked!

THE COURSE

Salt flats are not really as flat as they appear, but covered in buckles like a crumpled blanket. At Bonneville, the track where the car would run had to be prepared by towing a heavy drag behind a truck. This smoothed the course by scraping away all those pressure ridges. The salt grows daily as the high temperatures draw moisture through the surface – and constant dragging is needed to keep the track smooth. It was painstaking work, adding to the tension everybody felt, and what's more it cost thousands of dollars.

If the car ran off the smoothed track it would mean a bumpy ride. Particularly bad was driving over ruts that the metal wheels had dug on a previous run. Richard described this as 'like hitting the railway lines at Clapham Junction at two hundred and fifty miles an hour'.

But although there was no danger, that wasn't good enough. Richard needed to get the car going straight before he could even start to build his speed, let alone try for the record.

It was tricky because the team was getting impatient, but none of them knew what it was like for the driver. On airfields in Britain, Richard had been quite happy to use the afterburner and zip up to speeds of 260 m.p.h. Then, of course, this had been with rubber tyres on the car, which gave a better grip on the tarmac. But here, on the aluminium wheels, even though the terrain in theory was so much safer, he couldn't muster the confidence to do that.

A series of minor technical hitches added to the difficulties, and tempers began to fray. Behind Richard's back, people were putting the blame on him. 'If it's not the car, it must be the driver.' Richard could only urge them to persevere. He couldn't be sure there was anything that could be done to solve the problem, but one thing he was sure of: if they gave up now they were finished.

One night a storm almost blew the garage tent away. The whole team had to turn out in the dead of night to save it. But the experience helped a little. It defused some of the irritation that had been building up. From then on, the recriminations stopped and everyone just got on with doing their best.

It was 10 October 1982. *Thrust2* had undergone some minor adjustments to its suspension and was handling better. Richard went down the course at about 400 m.p.h. and felt he could do even better. He would have to do better if he was to beat the 403 m.p.h. British record held by the late Donald Campbell.

'We had decided to try our first turnaround – running the car straight back over the course – because the regulations stated that we would have to make two opposite direction runs within an hour for a record attempt to count.

'Well, everything went wrong. The fuel bowser broke the propshaft on its pump so we couldn't refuel. Then there was a delay getting the car towed into position. And all through it, the USAC time-keepers were counting away the minutes.

'Somehow we got away in the nick of time. I was so angry that I just thought, "stuff it!" and for the first time at Bonneville I kicked in the afterburner. I used it to the maximum. And we just went!

'I had worried that using the reheat might have made things worse, but miraculously I found that the extra power gave the car extra stability. Nobody had expected that; certainly I hadn't. In the cockpit I felt happy for the first time at Bonneville. We were really motoring. We got to a speed of around 500 m.p.h., my fastest ever, as I went into the measured mile. But the car was being so badly hammered by the rough surface that a battery connection worked loose. As I went into the mile I was actually decelerating as the engine lost

> power. It was a bit disappointing after the tremen-
> dous run-up, but we still came out with an average
> of 418.118 m.p.h.
>
> 'It was a new record. Thrust2 and I were the
> fastest-ever British car and driver. It wasn't the world
> record, but it was something. At last we had got our
> breakthrough.'
>
> — RICHARD NOBLE

There was no more time for running the car that afternoon, but Richard had high hopes for the next day. The team went off for a celebratory dinner in Wendover, the closest town to the salt flats. Everyone was in good spirits now. The meal was in full swing when somebody walked into the restaurant and they saw he was drenched.

Richard ran to the door. Outside it was pouring with rain.

By the next morning the flats were under two inches of water. The *Thrust2* crew were terribly disappointed. No sooner had they got going than they had been washed out.

Winter had come and there was no hope of

45

the course drying out again that year. There was nothing for it but to go back home.

Richard and his team had set an unofficial British record as the fastest ever car and driver. But if they were expecting a heroes' welcome, they were in for a rude awakening. Almost as soon as he'd flown in to Heathrow, Richard was summoned to meet the marketing director of Fabergé, one of the project's chief sponsors. He wasn't too impressed by their showing in Bonneville. 'Look here, Richard,' he said, 'you promised us gold and you only brought us back bronze.'

It was the same with the other sponsors. Money was needed to maintain the team and refurbish the car throughout the year until they could make another attempt at the record. At this stage, however, no-one seemed interested.

'There's one bit of good news,' Richard told the team. 'Before we left for Bonneville, we had spent our last thousand pounds insuring the desert against flooding. Our claim is worth £75,000, which should see us in good stead for next year's attempt.'

But Richard had a lot to learn about insurance companies. It looked as if they couldn't possibly refuse to pay out on the claim. After all, the BBC had televised everything in Bonneville, so it was obvious to the whole country that the salt flats had indeed flooded.

All the same, the insurance company refused to pay. 'You didn't make a record attempt,' they said.

Richard was furious. It was obvious that the insurance company had no intention of paying. So he had a meeting of all his sponsors and invited the director of the insurance brokers as well. He explained everything that had happened in Bonneville, summing up by saying that there would be nothing to prevent *Thrust2* winning the world record if they could only go back to Bonneville the next summer.

'I've called a press conference for ten days' time,' he told them.

'What are you going to say about the insurance?' asked the director of the brokers.

'That's very simple. If you pay up, we'll praise your company and say how grateful we are. If you still refuse to pay, I'll explain our very severe financial problems – and I'll personally hand out copies of your insurance policy to the media.'

The insurance director was horrified. 'You

wouldn't do that!'

'Oh yes we would,' said Richard.

Come the day of the press conference, the insurance director turned up with a leather wallet. It contained a cheque for £75,000. Richard and he shook hands while the press took their photographs.

The sponsors were happy too. They didn't mind investing a bit more money now that the project's finances were on a better footing. Everything looked rosy – but the team was about to suffer a setback that would very nearly end the project once and for all . . .

SIX

It was a beautiful summer's day at RAF
Greenham Common – the USAF air base near
Newbury in Berkshire. In a few months the dry
weather would return to Bonneville and they
could have another shot at the land speed
record. For today, Richard just needed to make
a few shakedown runs. Just routine, nothing
too challenging.

He hadn't driven *Thrust2* for a while since it
had been stripped down in the workshop
undergoing modifications. The idea of the
shakedown run was to get back into the swing
of things, to let Richard get used to the refitted
car.

The first day at Greenham Common was

wonderful. Richard had given a lot of people (including some key sponsors) 260 m.p.h. rides, which had gone well. The second seat in the car was proving useful. 'You could take the most unlikely people,' he remembers, 'strap them in and hurtle them down the runway at 260 m.p.h. It was brilliant.'

The following day was one of the worst of Richard's life. A day when just about everything went wrong.

Richard wasn't using the best brake parachutes, a cluster of three that the team knew as the Triple Ripple. The team wanted to save those for Bonneville. Instead the decision had been taken to run with the older brake 'chutes taken from a Phantom jet. Earlier in the day there had been a minor hitch with one of them that held up the low speed trials until the afternoon, but that had been fixed.

BRAKING

Trying to stop a high speed car causes a lot of heat in the brakes. This is caused by the speed energy which has to be lost before the car can stop.

Cars usually use wheel brakes to absorb this energy, and they do so by converting it to heat. This is all very well for normal vehicles at normal speeds, but ultra high-speed vehicles such as jet cars have too much energy to be safely dealt with by wheel brakes, so a braking parachute is used to stop from the highest speed. As the stopping force of a parachute falls dramatically with speed, it is usual to begin stopping with the parachute at high speed, and then use the wheel brakes at a lower speed where they are more effective than the parachute, but will not burn out from excessive energy.

They did one run without any problems and John Ackroyd said to Richard. 'As far as I'm concerned, the car's ready to go to Bonneville. Let's pack her up.'

'But Ackers, it's a lovely day. No crosswind. I'd like to get just one more run in before we go.'

That run wasn't strictly necessary as they had got all the data they needed. But Ackers knew that the driver was just as important as the car. If Richard felt he needed another run, so be it.

They lined the car up at the west end of the course. Mike Barratt, who was the team member in charge of the parachutes, took the passenger seat. When things went wrong, he and Richard were to get the ride of their lives.

It was late in the afternoon and Richard was getting tired. They were supposed to do only 200 m.p.h. but he kept his foot on the throttle a fraction too long. For a moment his attention drifted. There was a red Jaguar Firechase beside the course which Richard had been using as a visual cue to start ESD (engine shutdown). Somehow he missed it.

The first inkling that anything was wrong came when he saw smoke pouring off the front wheels. A puncture? It couldn't be – the car would have lost stability. Then what?

Whatever it was, he had his hands full with a jet car running out of control and the end of the runway coming up very fast indeed.

He shut the engine down and deployed the braking 'chute. It opened – and collapsed. Richard jumped on the brakes so hard that they locked up.

Everything was happening at once but he had to keep his wits. He was running out of runway and there was a deep quarry at the far end. The only thing for it was to swerve left on to the perimeter track. Should he fire the second 'chute and then turn with it deployed, or turn first and then try the 'chute?

He steered off the runway and the wheels

apexed a corner perfectly at about 200 m.p.h. He immediately put out the second 'chute. *Thrust2* ran on to the grass and started to slow.

There had been very little time for thinking, but luckily Richard made the right choice. Firing the second 'chute before the corner might have prevented them from turning the corner at all!

> 'What I hadn't done, which was unforgivable, was to walk the course before the run. What I imagined was flat grass, leading to a large concrete pan where I could brake hard, was actually rough and bumpy. We ploughed into it and clouds of muck and stones went flying into the engine intake.
>
> 'We had shredded the front tyres when I'd locked up the wheels for a thousand metres and all the turf and stones went flying everywhere, and we ground to a halt just before we ran out of space.'
>
> — RICHARD NOBLE

Richard and Mike Barratt ripped off their seatbelts and jumped out. As a crowd of onlookers came running over, they surveyed the damage. The whole front of the car was severely damaged from the impact with the ground. Far worse was the state of the engine now it had ingested stones and turf from Greenham Common.

Ackers was furious. He stormed off and it was a week before Richard saw him again, when the whole team gathered for a meeting. It was almost a post mortem, since many were convinced that *Thrust2* would never run again.

Ackers explained what had happened. Richard had allowed *Thrust2* to get up to nearly 300 m.p.h., at which point the tyres expanded so much owing to centrifugal force that they began to rub against the bodywork. That was the source of the smoke Richard had seen. It was friction rubbing the tyres away.

And that wasn't the only problem. Although Richard thought he had shut the engine down when he saw the smoke, he had actually only got it to idle. It was still pushing against the brakes even when they had got onto the grass.

'The damage to the bodywork alone will take months to rebuild,' said Ackers. 'That will take us right up to Bonneville. And that's assuming we can get a new engine.'

The engine had been removed the night of the accident at Greenham and sent straight up to RAF Binbrook so that the team's Avon expert, John Watkins, could look at it. 'I've never seen one so badly damaged,' he told them on the phone. 'The stones have made a real mess of the compressor blades. It'll cost a fortune to rebuild it!'

Obviously there were some of the team who thought Richard should step down as driver – if the project had any chance at all of continuing now. There was a long hard discussion. Richard agreed that he needed more training and more self-discipline. With *Thrust2* out of action he took an instruments-only flying course to hone his reflexes.

He had learned a lot from that spill at Greenham Common. Even as he put in his flying hours he was determined he would never again make another stupid mistake like that.

A few weeks later he had a call from John Watkins at RAF Binbrook. 'You made a right mess of that engine!'

Richard groaned. 'I know, everyone's told me the same thing.'

'Well, I want to know what we should do with it now.'

'John, it would cost two hundred quid just to send a truck to collect it. It'll be easier if you just scrap it.'

'Scrap?' John laughed. 'But we've fixed it. It's ready to go back in the car!'

Richard was almost speechless. The engineers at RAF Binbrook had rebuilt the engine, as he was to discover, to a better specification than it had been originally. They had worked in the evenings and at nights, using RAF parts, with approval. And they had done it for nothing.

So the accident at Greenham Common, which had looked like such a disaster on the day, had led to a new discipline for team and driver, and a rebuilt and improved jet.

There was only one snag still to overcome. The repairs to the bodywork took twelve weeks, overrunning the time they had booked on the course at Bonneville. The next slot on the course had been booked by Don Vesco, one of the legendary stars of Bonneville racing history who was planning an attack on the motorcycle speed record. Don spoke to Richard on the phone and very graciously agreed to share the time he had booked on the flats. It was now the middle of September 1982 and they were set to go.

The second time *Thrust2* was loaded onto a plane bound for the glaring white salt of

Bonneville, it was a greatly improved vehicle. As well as the upgraded engine, Ackers had opted for six-inch-wide front wheels in place of the four-inch units used the previous time. There had also been revisions to the front suspension to give the steering more self-centring and better feel.

During the flight from Heathrow the whole team felt confident. On their earlier visit to Bonneville it was only bad luck that had kept them from attempting the record.

But their share of bad luck hadn't been used up yet. As they drove towards Bonneville, there were black storm clouds ahead. In place of the enormous white expanse of the salt flats they found a grey-blue lake.

'We can go swimming,' said Richard, 'but it doesn't look like there'll be any driving.'

They had salvaged the project from the brink of extinction after Greenham Common. They had been given time on the salt by Don Vesco. They had shipped everything six thousand miles across the Atlantic. And now they were rained out. Beaten – or so it seemed – even before they had a chance to unload the car.

SEVEN

On the evening of 28 September 1982, the *Thrust* team gathered for dinner at the Stateline Casino in Wendover. Listening to the rain hissing down outside took them back to the last time they'd been here.

'The difference this time,' Richard said, 'is that we're not going back to Britain without the land speed record.'

'Are you sure you don't mean the water speed record?' said someone. Nobody laughed.

'What we need is a minimum of twenty kilometres that is flat, dry, relatively free of stones, and devoid of plant life,' said Ken Norris, the team manager.

Peter Moore, a friend of Richard's, who had

dropped by to watch the car in action, had a suggestion. 'Has anybody heard of the Black Rock Desert in Nevada?'

It turned out that Richard had marked out Black Rock as a back-up venue two years earlier. He still hadn't visited it to take a look in person, but now that the salt flats were washed out there was nothing else on offer.

They drove across from Utah to Nevada, approaching the Black Rock Desert cross-country via the dirt road from Winnemucca that brings you out at the ghost town of Sulphur on the eastern side. As soon as they came across the railway line there and saw the massive yellow-brown mud flats known as playa stretched out in front of them, they knew they'd struck gold.

Richard got out of the car. 'This is it!' he cried.

All that would have to be done was the defodding – a painstaking process that involved walking down the course picking up any pebbles or small objects that might get sucked up to damage the jet intake. The surface was so flat that there wasn't even any need to drag it like Bonneville. And if the car got loose, there were miles and miles of run-off area in which it could slow down.

'We ran Thrust2 on Bonneville in 1981 – with not very encouraging results. Because of its very high speed, Thrust2 had to use solid wheels without tyres, just like ThrustSSC. The solid wheels did not like the hard Bonneville salt and the car was never comfortably stable.

'In 1982, the Thrust2 team tried to run at Bonneville again, but the day we arrived, winter came and the desert flooded. By sheer good fortune we discovered the Black Rock Desert in Nevada, which was still dry, but which has a different surface. Instead of the white salt this was a light-brown alkali hard baked surface made from millions of tons of alluvia washed down from the nearby Sierra Nevada Mountains. But there was a crucial difference – the Black Rock surface had a hard crust with a softer mud surface below – and that springy mud made the surface a bit like a mattress – the springy bit made an ideal fit with the hard solid wheels. Put simply, the special Black Rock surface did the job of the tyres. Thrust2 handled really well on the Black Rock Surface – and the rest is history!'

— RICHARD NOBLE

They went into the nearby town of Gerlach, where a signpost told them the population was three hundred and fifty, and met Bruno Selmi, the owner of the only motel there. To his delight they booked all his rooms and lost no time getting their gear moved across from Bonneville.

Richard's first test run confirmed his hopes. The playa was smooth and felt a lot safer to drive on than the salt flats. And it was most certainly flat. In fact, Ackers calculated that *Thrust2* had a rougher ride on its trailer at 30 m.p.h. than it would while travelling under its own power at over 500 m.p.h. The sole concern, apart from some patches of the playa that were still a little damp from recent rain, was that the dusty surface had greater rolling resistance than Bonneville's hard salt. They considered that a reasonable trade-off, given that the greater stability of the surface would make it possible for them to use all of *Thrust2*'s power for the first time.

*

If you push an object, in the absence of any other forces, it will keep on accelerating in the direction you're pushing it. Even a thrust of a newton would eventually move a million-tonne weight across the galaxy, just as long as no other forces such as friction were applied against it.

So with several thousand newtons of thrust, what other forces were holding *Thrust2* back? There were two: drag and rolling resistance.

Drag is the resistance due to the air. This increases with the square of the speed up to supersonic speeds. Rolling resistance is caused by the characteristics of the wheels and the surface they're in contact with. It may increase as you get faster, but not in the simple square-law way that subsonic drag does.

What happens is that *Thrust2* starts to accelerate and, as it gains speed, the forces holding it back also increase – until eventually the drag and rolling resistance are equal to the thrust of the engine, at which point the car would be at its maximum speed.

So to break the land speed record you need to:

•Acquire the most powerful afterburning jet engine you can find.

Within a month, *Thrust2*'s speed was up to 575 m.p.h. and on 4 November 1982 Richard went beyond 600 m.p.h. for the first time while setting an average over the mile of 590.551.

It was a new record for British car and driver, but still the world record proved elusive and now the weather was closing in. The course was damp, adding to rolling drag, and with winter on the way there was little prospect for improvement.

The technicians pressed the car for ever more power while everyone else prayed for a hot spell to dry the ground. It didn't come. Winter, and deep snow, was just days away.

So it was back to England after all. But this time they didn't return in near disgrace, as they had the year before. Now they had proven

Thrust2's capabilities and were in with a chance. Another insurance claim against the winter weather that had finally sent them packing was settled, this time without dispute.

The Avon 302 engine was bench-tested at Rolls-Royce, East Kilbride. The results were promising, but it was clear they would have only one more crack at the record. The sponsors were not going to keep pumping money in indefinitely.

So by the end of August 1983 they were back at the Black Rock Desert. This was *Thrust2*'s last chance. Within a fortnight Richard was surpassing the speeds he had achieved the first time.

To try and push the speed up even more, Ackers suggested running in the middle of the day. Up to then, the runs had been made early in the day. This was when the air was cool and dense, which meant that the engine produced greater power but also the aerodynamic drag was greater. Higher temperatures would mean lower transonic drag – but less engine power.

That trade-off worked out more in their favour at noon. The lower drag at that time of day allowed the team to edge *Thrust2* to 617 m.p.h. The record set by Gary Gabelich with his rocket-powered *Blue Flame* in 1970 was 622.407 m.p.h., so they were snapping at his heels.

But Richard's concern now was that *Thrust2* had reached a performance plateau. To snatch the record, they needed even more power to raise the speed through the measured mile. Instead the Avon engine was acting up because it was being oversped. During one run the jet pipe temperature suddenly shot up to record levels, forcing Richard to abort the scheduled return run.

The fear was that the engine might be surging, ingesting too much air until pressure built up and it began blasting it forwards out of the intake. This not only could result in loss of thrust, it could severely damage the compressor.

There was no-one in the desert with anything like the expertise needed to do a full check of a jet engine. John Watkins, their engine specialist, was unable to get away from RAF Binbrook. He couldn't tell them much over the phone; he needed to see the engine for himself. What they really needed was help from Rolls-Royce.

Richard pulled one of his inspired acts of desperation. He gave an exclusive interview to the *Financial Times* in which he referred to the difficulties with the engine. Then he faxed the chairman of Rolls-Royce saying, 'We can get this record, except the engine is letting us down. It may only be an installation problem that's easy to fix, but we need someone to show us what to do. If you decide not to help, I quite understand, but then there'll be no point in continuing and we'll have to come home.'

The reply came quickly. It was largely what Richard expected – the chairman was not at all happy. Many people on the board of directors saw what the *Thrust* team was doing as an unofficial and unapproved installation of one of their engines. But at the end of a very angry fax, he relented. Rolls-Royce would send an expert to Nevada.

George Webb duly arrived and lost no time in climbing inside the jet pipe to see for himself. 'There's none of the metal spatter that would indicate internal trouble. And if you'd had a surge, you'd certainly know about it,' he said. 'It was just a simple flame-out.'

This was a great relief, but there was more good news to come. 'The afterburner control linkage isn't connected properly,' he discovered. 'You haven't been using the fourth and final section of the reheat.'

'Do you mean,' said Richard, 'that all this time I've been running the car, we've never had full power?'

It was exhilarating news. Once George Webb had altered the connections, *Thrust2* would have an extra spring in its step. That extra boost was all they needed to leave Gary Gabelich's record behind in the dust.

Just to make absolutely sure, Ackers did everything he could to minimize drag. To smooth the airflow, he fitted small deflectors on the underside of the car ahead of the front wheels. The paintwork and underside were rubbed down and polished to a mirror finish, so that drag would be reduced to a minimum.

There was one more change he wanted to make, but for this he needed Richard's consent.

Up until then, *Thrust2* had been running with the front and back of the car at the same height above the ground. In that configuration, when running at 623 m.p.h. there was a downforce of 2885 kilograms on the front wheels. This was 10% higher than the static weight, the difference being due to the aerodynamic down-force. Effectively, the car was acting like a wing in reverse: the faster it got, the more it was pushed down by the airflow. The trouble with this was that it tended to make the front wheels plough into the ground, increasing the car's rolling resistance.

What Ackers wanted to do was raise the front ride height by a fraction. And when he said a fraction, he meant that literally – the proposed change was an increased angle of a few hundredths of a degree.

Richard was worried. Craig Breedlove's *Spirit of America* had lifted its front wheels clear of the ground at 600 m.p.h. It was every driver's fear that his car would start to fly.

Ackers patiently went through the calculations. 'At 650 m.p.h. you'd have aerodynamic lift of 925 kg. Since the static weight of the car is 2613 kg, you'll still have 1688 kg keeping you firmly in contact with Mother Earth.'

'I was uncomfortable about raising the front of the car even a small bit. The weight can come off very quickly as you increase speed. It's because the lift moves the nose up just a little more, increasing the angle of attack, and that gives a bit more lift – it's positive feedback. If the underside of the car is exposed to the near-supersonic airflow, the car will fly with terrifying results.

> '*I never forgot the sight of Donald Campbell's fatal somersault on Coniston Water. I let Ackers make the adjustment, but I knew the system we had for measuring load on the front suspension was fairly crude. Really it was mainly guesswork.*'
>
> — RICHARD NOBLE

The fourth of October brought a beautiful dawn, and many of the team said later that they somehow knew *Thrust2* would take the record that day.

Richard felt no such thing. He'd got to the point where the runs were routine, and he was taking nothing for granted.

The day wore on and the temperature crept up into the low seventies. There was no wind. It was ideal for a run, but there was yet one more nerve-stretching moment at 14:45p.m. when a fuse failed in the ignition. The electrician made a desperate run south across the desert to the far end of the course for a replacement. Strapped in the sweltering cockpit, Richard felt those minutes were the longest wait of the whole nine-year project that had got him to this point.

The electrician fitted the new fuse. The engine

was started and Richard was given the signal to go.

He accelerated into the measured mile and got a speed of 624.241 m.p.h. It was just faster than Gary Gabelich's record. But that was not enough. To set a new record, Richard had to complete two runs within one hour and the average speed of these runs had to exceed Gabelich's speed by at least 1% (6 1/4 m.p.h.).

The team turned *Thrust2* around and set out on the return run. This time he was starting from the firmer end of the course, which meant better acceleration from the outset.

Richard stopped after the second run and waited for the timekeepers to announce the speed. When it came he gave a great shout of joy and triumph. After all the effort and heartache they'd made it.

The speed was 642.971 m.p.h. The average of the two passes gave Britain a new World Land Speed Record – 633.468 m.p.h. – the first in nineteen years.

As the crew relaxed into their victory party, a television reporter asked Richard what had motivated him to go for the land speed record in the first place.

'For Britain,' said Richard; then he thought again and added: 'And for the hell of it.'

Part 2

FASTER THAN SOUND

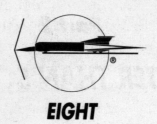

EIGHT

It was to be 1990 before Richard returned to Bonneville, this time not as a driver but as a journalist.

Art Arfons had built a new version of his classic *Green Monster* jet car – his twenty-seventh – and at the age of sixty was intending to have a stab at Richard's land speed record. Naturally Richard was curious to see how he fared.

There are regular hot-rod meets at Bonneville, so while Arfons was running his *Green Monster* there were many other exotic land-speed vehicles around. And, because a television documentary was being made about Art Arfons' life, his old friend Craig Breedlove showed up as well.

Richard got talking to Breedlove and was amazed to hear he was working on a new car of his own. Breedlove had been the first man to exceed 400 m.p.h. in 1963, and the first to go faster than 500 m.p.h. and then 600 m.p.h. in the following two years. Now, after a gap of twenty-five years, he was making a spectacular comeback. He had to be aiming at the 700 m.p.h. record – and after that it was a logical assumption that he would try for the speed of sound (also known as Mach 1).

Richard, for his part, had been out of the land speed record business for seven years. It was sort of an enforced retirement, because his sponsors weren't interested in backing him just to beat his own record. But with Craig Breedlove's new project, there would come a lot of media attention – and the possibility of a race, which would bring the sponsors back for a new *Thrust* car.

Richard had always intended to build a third car and he had looked at a number of ways of doing it. But he was concerned by several factors, of which the most important was the question of aerodynamic lift. After the *Thrust2* record run, Ackers had calculated that at its peak speed it only needed to have gone about

seven miles per hour faster before the front end
would have lifted and the car would have been
hurled vertically upwards in a totally uncon-
trolled manner.

In addition, if the new car was to break the
sound barrier, it would have to be designed to
withstand the extreme and dangerous turbu-
lence experienced as the speed of sound is
approached.

BREAKING THE SOUND BARRIER

There is, in fact, no such thing as a 'sound barrier'.
This is a phrase coined at a time when it seemed
that there would never be any possibility of any
vehicle being able to travel faster than the speed of
sound – it seemed to be a 'barrier' through which
mankind would never be able to break. It was a
catchy phrase, however, and it has stuck in
people's minds ever since.

Perhaps the reason the phrase has stuck for so
long is that it presents a simple image. The reality
of getting a vehicle to go supersonic (faster than the
speed of sound) is much more complicated.

Think about the flow of air around a vehicle travelling at high speed. In forward-facing regions,
such as in front of the wheels and in front of the

cockpit canopy, the airflow is slowed down. In contrast, there are other regions, such as over the top of the canopy or the bulbous parts of the engine cowlings, where the flow of air is speeded up. So, if the vehicle is travelling at or near the speed of sound (this is called the transonic region), there will be some areas where the airflow is travelling more slowly, while in other places the flow will already be supersonic.

If the vehicle accelerates to a slightly higher speed, there will be fewer regions of its surface experiencing subsonic (below the speed of sound) flow and more regions experiencing supersonic flow. Also the shock waves (the boundaries between supersonic flow and subsonic flow) will get stronger and will move. As a result, every time the vehicle changes speed, the forces change and the attitude (the angle at which the vehicle cuts through the air) may need to be adjusted.

And there are further hidden dangers in this transonic region. The local areas of subsonic flow and supersonic flow act as if they are vying for supremacy. In some circumstances, the flow pattern can become unstable and the rapidly changing forces can vibrate the structure dangerously.

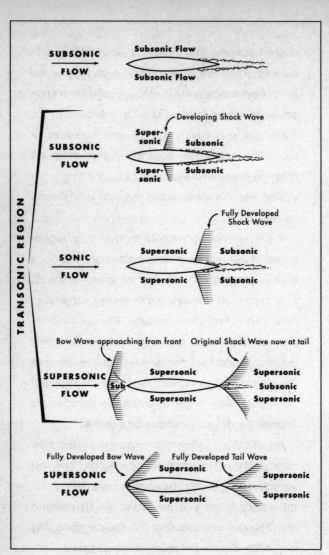

How Shock Waves Form

Clearly the new car called for the skills of an ace aerodynamicist who could devise the perfect design. Also, the design would need to undergo very thorough research before the car itself could be built.

Richard spent the next year or so trying to drum up interest. He needed a lucky break to get the ball rolling, and in July 1992 he got it when he met a man called Ron Ayers.

Ron had worked as chief aerodynamicist on missiles for the British Aircraft Corporation and, in particular, on the Bloodhound 2 anti-aircraft missile. Now retired, he was researching land speed record car aerodynamics.

'One thing that bothers me,' he said to Richard: 'looking at the design and power of all the fastest cars, it's obvious they're under-performing. They just aren't getting the speed they should. I've a feeling it's the wheels.' He suggested that the rolling resistance was always higher than anyone expected it to be.

Ron did his calculations and was able to show that at 650 m.p.h. there was a difference of several thousand newtons between the force of the Avon engine pushing *Thrust2* forward and the drag due to air resistance holding it back.

Was all that power absorbed by the rolling resistance of the Black Rock Desert?

As Richard and Ron discussed the idea of a supersonic car, they agreed that before they could even consider such a thing, they had to know exactly what had been happening with *Thrust2*. But once they had done some initial work, Richard realized that they couldn't get any further without some funding for more research. Then he had another stroke of luck.

Castrol's marketing and technology director got wind of Richard's plans and it was agreed that Castrol would be the new car's first sponsor. They would start things off with an investment of £40,000 to cover research into the new design.

Now that the project had got started, it needed a name. Richard's original plan, all those years before when he was starting out, had been to use *Thrust2* to raise money and then build another car, *Thrust3*, to break the land speed record. But *Thrust2* had turned out to be good enough for the task in its own right. Should he call this new car *Thrust3*, or was it time to break the mould?

He decided to call it *ThrustSSC*, standing for

Supersonic Car. The new name indicated a fresh start. Also, it had the virtue that it told people straightaway what the aim was. This wasn't just another record-breaking car. This one was going to be designed to break the sound barrier.

It was going to be something very different from the *Thrust* vehicles that had gone before.

DESIGNING A SUPERSONIC CAR

One of the biggest questions a designer is faced with at the beginning is one of layout. Where should the engine, the driver and the fuel be put? Ideally, the driver should be near the centre of the car to give him the best 'seat-of-the-pants' feel for the vehicle's movements. It is also easier to protect the driver if there is plenty of structure around him.

The fuel tank should also be near the centre of the vehicle so that as the fuel is used up during a run and the tank empties, the change in weight doesn't make a significant difference to the vehicle's centre of gravity.

The engine has got to lie on the centre-line of the vehicle and, being such a large and heavy item, is bound to occupy the centre, as well.

Figure A shows the slender-body solution adopted by the early builders of jet cars. The big advantage these cars had was that the shape was very slender and aerodynamic. The position of the fuel tank was not too bad, but the driver was positioned so far forward that he could get very little 'feel' for what was happening at the back of the car. The most serious problem was one of stability. In order to minimize the vehicle's potential to roll over, slide sideways or tip up at high speeds, several compromises had to be made about the position of the centre of gravity, none of them particularly satisfactory. When *Spirit of America* rolled onto its side in 1996, the difficulties with this general layout were clearly demonstrated.

John Cobb's CRUSADER hydrofoil on Loch Ness –
Richard Noble's first inspiration.

Donald Campbell's fatal accident on Coniston Water
shows the dangers of aerodynamic lift.

Thrust1.

An inelegant end for Thrust1...

One of the first steps towards Thrust2 – the arrival of a Rolls-Royce turbojet engine at Richard Noble's house.

Thrust2 takes shape at Fishbourne, Isle of Wight (1980).

Thrust2 engine tests at Fallon Naval Base, Nevada (1982).

Richard Noble, ready for the record attempt in Thrust2.

Setting the world land speed record! October 1983

A 1/25 scale model of ThrustSSC was tested to Mach 1.15 using this Rocket Sled.

ThrustSSC has two massive Rolls-Royce Spey 202 engines.

An early static test demonstrates the sheer power of ThrustSSC's engines.

Squadron Leader Andy Green with ThrustSSC.

The ThrustSSC cockpit.

ThrustSSC runs for the first time on the Al Jafr desert in Jordan (1996).

A gentle start – to prevent the car hoovering up the desert!

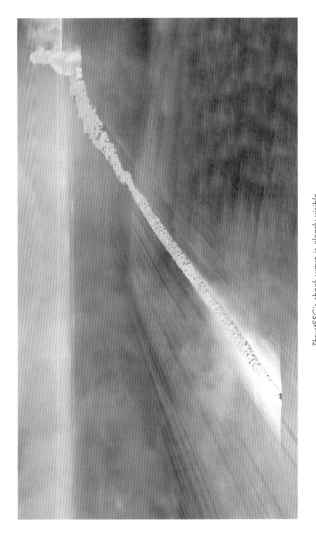

ThrustSSC's shock wave is clearly visible, fanning out from the front wheels.

The ThrustSSC team.

Jack Noble celebrates the record-breaking run.

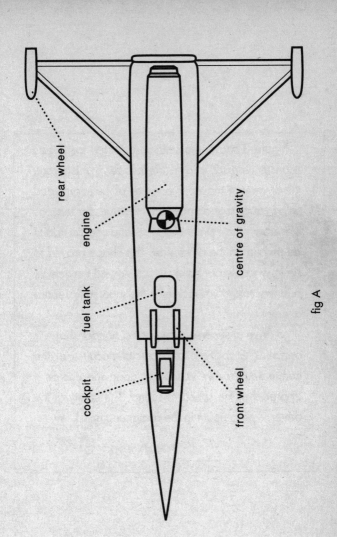

rear wheel

engine

centre of gravity

fuel tank

cockpit

front wheel

fig A

Figure B shows the solution adopted for *Green Monster*, *Thrust2*, and *Aussie Invader*. In this layout, the driver was moved to one side of the engine and was in quite a good position. However, for reasons of aerodynamic symmetry, a second cockpit had to be placed on the other side. This shape proved to be very stable but bulky, which slowed the vehicle and was totally unsuitable for the supersonic record attempt.

To drive at supersonic speeds a slender shape is essential. Stability is also crucial because of the tremendous forces which act upon the car as it approaches the speed of sound. The safety of the driver is paramount in the designer's mind.

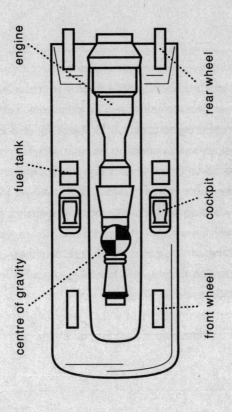

engine

rear wheel

fuel tank

centre of gravity

cockpit

front wheel

fig B

Figure C shows how all of these were achieved in *ThrustSSC*. With a two-engine layout, the centre of the car is made available for the driver and for the fuel, as well as enabling the front wheels to be placed wide apart. This design, by putting the heaviest parts of car forward and between the widely-spaced front wheels, stops any tendency to roll. With the weight well forward and the fins well back, the car is stable, like a dart. Together, all these design factors were to make it possible for *ThrustSSC* to go supersonic.

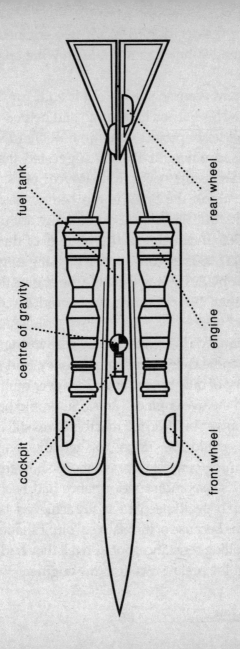

fuel tank

rear wheel

centre of gravity

engine

cockpit

front wheel

fig C

Once the decision to go for two engines had been made, they had to settle on what engines to use.

Richard went to see his old friend, Air Chief Marshal Sir Patrick Hine, who had helped with the *Thrust2* project. At first Richard was surprised when Sir Patrick suggested that he should consider using Rolls-Royce Speys.

'You think the Spey is too heavy,' said Sir Patrick. 'But I'll bet you don't know about the Spey 205. It can give 25,000 pounds of thrust – that's 111,000 newtons – and it has single crystal turbine blades that will enable the engine to run at higher temperatures and produce more power.'

Richard didn't take much convincing. He made some calls, spent some money, and soon had two of only twelve Spey 205s ever built.

With the two engines *ThrustSSC* would have a lot of power, but Ron felt that there was still more which could be done to get the engines performing better. His calculations showed that *Thrust2*'s maximum performance had been the 650 m.p.h. peak speed it actually achieved. Partly that was because of its relatively blunt shape and high rolling resistance, but Ron felt they had also not got the best results from the engine.

Part of the problem is that the air entering the jet engine of a vehicle travelling at high speeds has to be slowed down first. If the air was left to zoom through unchecked, it would pass through the engine at such a high speed that a steady flame would never be achieved. This vital process of slowing down the air is begun by incorporating a cleverly designed air intake in the front of the engine.

Using data provided by Ian McGregor (the intake design specialist at DERA, the Defence Evaluation and Research Agency), Ron designed long air intakes for *ThrustSSC* which slowed the air down very efficiently.

The Speys have an 'air by-pass' where some of the compressed air is passed around the combustion chamber and into the afterburners. This increases the amount of unburned air in the afterburners, allowing more fuel to be burned there; as the amount of air increases with an increase in vehicle speed, the engine thrust also increases as the car goes faster.

This design had an enormous advantage over a pure turbojet. And the Thrust team would need every advantage they could get.

NINE

By now, Richard and Ron were getting very excited about *ThrustSSC*, but even though the engines were sorted out and the design was starting to shape up, they still hadn't solved every problem. Richard had a well-found fear that the supersonic shock-waves under the car might cause it to fly, which is why many of the previous high speed cars had a slim, deep V-shape underneath. But Ron had designed *ThrustSSC* to be flat underneath,

'Surely this shape is not right,' Richard protested.

'Just because nobody has tried it before doesn't mean it's not right,' said Ron. 'Nobody has tested what happens under a car at super-sonic speed. Before we finalize our design, we're going to have to find out.'

How were they going to do that? Although wind tunnels did exist that had moving ground to simulate the conditions under the car, none of them could operate at transonic or supersonic speeds. The reason for this is that wind tunnels equipped to simulate the ground moving under a vehicle do so with a belt that runs on a continuous loop under the scale model being tested. If you run the belt at speeds much beyond 100 m.p.h., it gets sucked up towards the model and the team needed to be able to test the design at speeds up to 800 m.p.h.

One immediate solution was to use computational fluid dynamics – CFD for short. CFD is a computer analysis method which enables the airflow around the vehicle to be simulated.

Professor Ken Morgan's team at Swansea University had developed one such CFD program, called *Flite*.

'You have to understand that the computer is modelling the airflow as millions of tiny particles,' said Ron, having talked to the professor. 'Each particle has to satisfy five simultaneous equations with all surrounding particles. The computer will have to crunch through umpteen different iterations until it settles down.'

'How long will the calculations take, then?'

'To give you some idea, just one picture – one "virtual snapshot" at a given speed – will take the university computer seven days to calculate.'

The problem was that Swansea University didn't have a fast enough computer for this exceptionally complex program. They made contact with the Cray Corporation, who agreed to loan the use of a Cray Supercomputer capable of running five billion calculations a second. Instead of seven days, each 'virtual snapshot' was ready in just seven hours.

So they had the data from the CFD analysis with which to refine and finalize the prototype design of *ThrustSSC*. But, just as with any computational model, the results of CFD were really just a good starting point. Professor Morgan's *Flite* software had been proved accurate to within 4% for aeroplanes flying at 30,000 feet, but it had never been used for testing a vehicle on the ground before. It was to provide extremely valuable data, which would enable them to prove the case.

If the CFD data was correct, the design of *ThrustSSC* worked in theory. Now they needed to test it in reality.

It was obvious that they couldn't use a wind tunnel, so Richard said, 'If we can't have a static model and moving air, let's have a mobile model and static air.'

Years earlier he had heard about the rocket test track at the Proof & Experimental Establishment at Pendine in Wales. There are several rocket test tracks around the world, mostly used for testing missile warheads and bombs. Some in America could accelerate a warhead up to Mach 9. Pendine ran to Mach 3.2, which was more than enough for *ThrustSSC*'s requirements.

Pendine's superintendent, Colonel Lowry, understood that Richard didn't have any money to pay for expensive tests. 'We're interested in your project,' he said, 'and we'll help you in any way we can.'

The rocket track comprised two parallel railway lines, 1.6 kilometres long, and the astounding thing is that it is straight and parallel across that distance to within 0.6 millimetres. Normally it is used to shoot bombs and missiles at over three times the speed of sound. They come off the end and slam into concrete targets.

Although the test requirements for *ThrustSSC* were very different, the rocket sled could be adapted to carry a $1/25$th scale model of *ThrustSSC* on a probe which pointed out ahead of it. Ron arranged for the centre section of the track to be filled in to represent the desert surface. The instrumented model would pass over the 'desert' surface at supersonic speed and provide valuable data at subsonic, transonic and supersonic speeds. With each of the thirteen test runs they would acquire data for every step of the acceleration and deceleration.

The first time they ran it, Richard was amazed. One moment he was looking at the model on its sled, the next instant the rockets fired and it was almost as though the model had vanished. It had accelerated at incredible velocity, racing past in front of him at supersonic speed.

'The Thrust2 car had reached a peak speed of 650.88 m.p.h. and had nearly flown. With the ThrustSSC project we would be pushing deep into the dangerous transonic range and the safety and stability of the car would be crucial. To understand what would happen to ThrustSSC at these speeds, we decided to run rocket models to supersonic speeds with the help of the DERA teams at Pendine in South Wales. We built a series of $1/25$th scale models of ThrustSSC which were heavily instrumented and mounted on the front of a rocket sled, which was powered by 18 solid fuel rocket motors. Once ignited the rocket and model would accelerate quickly to 1.2 times the speed of sound – and at the mid point of the track the model would race across a specially prepared surface with its wheels just 1mm from the test surface. The electronic instruments mounted in the model would record all the air pressures around the model and send the data via a radio link to the main computers for storage.

'On one of the first runs the model and sled accelerated well to supersonic speeds, but the carbon fibre model bodywork was very slightly damaged. We made the repair and sent the model down the track to Mach 1.2 a few days later. It accelerated

> *from 0–820 m.p.h. in 0.8 of a second. I was horri-*
> *fied to find that the model had disintegrated into a*
> *million pieces at Mach 1.2. The supersonic airflow*
> *had somehow burst into the model at the repair*
> *point – and then blown it into a zillion pieces. This*
> *was a terrible lesson. If any part of the fullscale*
> *ThrustSSC bodywork were faulty, then the super-*
> *sonic airflow would destroy the huge car – just as*
> *it had destroyed the model. No driver could survive*
> *that accident. It was to haunt me throughout the*
> *project.'*
>
> *— RICHARD NOBLE*

Comparing the results from the rocket tests with the CFD data showed a near perfect match over a wide range of possible conditions. It was the confirmation they needed. The design would work. They had the green light.

They were all was delighted. 'Now,' Richard said, 'let's build it.'

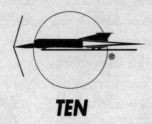

TEN

There was no time to lose. Craig Breedlove was also working on a supersonic car and, if he beat the Thrust team to the punch, Richard had no doubt that he'd lose his sponsors overnight. Nobody would care about the second car to go faster than sound.

Castrol was providing some of the money, of course, and many other companies were helping out by providing labour or components for nothing. But Richard still needed to find another £50,000 each month.

Nor was finance the only problem. The decision to go ahead with the build had forced the team to consider a whole range of new factors. The mechanical and structural design

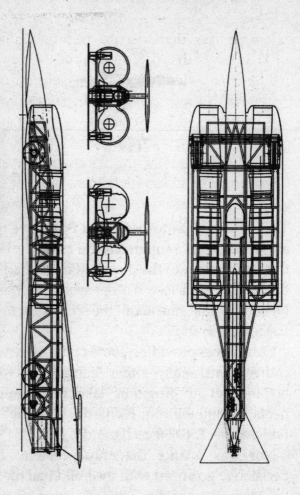

This diagram shows how Glynne's chassis structure
fitted in beneath ThrustSSC's exterior

had been completed by Glynne Bowsher and now all the detailed systems of the car had to be fitted.

Something that Richard had noticed with *Thrust2* was that a great deal of the valuable time on the desert had been spent on maintenance. The new car would have to be easy to strip down, all its systems easy to get at and quick to change if necessary. They couldn't afford to have something like an aeroplane with dozens of little service hatches all over it. So instead they decided to use a steel structure, with the engines mounted on either side and a skin made of carbon, aluminium and titanium.

As a result, *ThrustSSC* was going to be heavy, but with the twin Spey engines it was also overpowered. This was good because it meant that the weight of the car really didn't matter – weight restricts acceleration, not speed, and with two engines they would have all the acceleration they needed. It allowed what Ron called a 'belt and braces' approach whereby they would have a lot of leeway in other aspects of the design.

Then, one day in 1994, Glynne Bowsher rang Richard with a bombshell.

'Look, Richard, I am having problems with

the front wheel installation; there is neither the space to steer them nor structure to hang them on to, and there are other difficulties too. Now, one option is to increase the diameter of the nacelles substantially to get around this . . .'

Richard saw what was coming. 'But that will put the drag up.'

'Quite.' Glynne unleashed his bombshell: 'The only answer is to put the steering in the rear wheels.'

Richard's immediate thoughts were of un-controllable supermarket trolleys and everything else he could think of with rear-wheel steering was unstable too.

'The main reason to go with rear-wheel steering was the two big air intakes for the jets. They took up most of the room where the support structure for suspension and steering would be expected to go.

'But it was much more than that. The weight and speed range of the car gave wheel problems with the gyroscopic couples and also bearings and brakes. Those wheels were too heavy and wide and were going to rotate at over 8000 revolutions

> *per minute. Any attempt at steering them at high speed would result in the generation of a gyroscopic force couple which would try to roll the car. This is minimized by steering the lighter rear wheels, but most important of all, this arrangement solved all the problems with the front wheels.'*
>
> — *GLYNNE BOWSHER: Mechanical Designer*

Richard was still sceptical, so Glynne set out to prove his point using a converted Mini! His brother-in-law had abandoned the Mini in a field and Glynne rescued it from oblivion. He locked the front wheels in a straight-ahead position. Then, to give it the same wheelbase to track ratio as *ThrustSSC*, he built a long space-frame on to the back which incorporated two steering wheels in the same 'tandem offset' arrangement as the full-size vehicle. In fact the Mini wheelplan was a scale model of that of *ThrustSSC*.

Mini blueprint

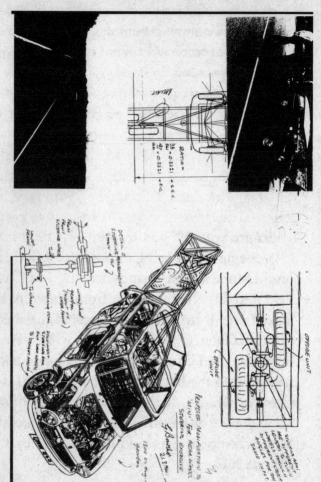

With some trepidation they took it to the MIRA (Motor Industries Research Association) test track at Nuneaton. The manager of the track took one look and said, 'What on earth are you doing?'

Richard tested the Mini on the straight and at first it was all over the place. It seemed to confirm his worst fears about rear wheel steering. When going into a corner, he had to be thinking about getting the back out in one direction in order to turn the opposite way. He found it confusing and the car was swerving all over the place.

'It's not going to work, Glynne,' said Richard after a few test laps.

Glynne was beavering away under the car. 'There's a bit of a slip in the linkage.' He tightened it up. 'Try it again.'

Richard grumbled but agreed to give it a go. This time the Mini performed like magic. He found he could take the straights at 90 m.p.h., with his hands off the wheel, and not swerve an inch. The corners he could handle at 40 m.p.h. with no difficulty.

Richard got out after the test and shook Glynne's hand. 'You're a genius, Glynne. It really works!'

Glynne gave a modest smile. 'Of course it does,' he said.

So in the space of two years the team had done all the aerodynamic research, developed the design for a supersonic car, acquired the jet engines, drawn up the spaceframe structure, and now they were well on their way towards building it.

But they still needed one thing: the right man to drive it.

ELEVEN

There are two ways of selecting someone for a job. If it's an ordinary job you can find someone who's doing the job already. If they're highly regarded in their profession, if they have a good track record, they're probably worth hiring. Or you can look for the qualities the job requires, which usually means hiring someone who has the right qualifications – exam results, character and aptitude.

It gets much harder in the case of a job that nobody has ever done before. Driving a super-sonic car, for instance. Then you have to decide what characteristics a person might need in order to do that job well. Inevitably there's an element of guesswork.

Someone commented to Richard that the obvious thing was to give any applicants a sanity test. Anyone who failed would be a prime candidate for driving *ThrustSSC*! It was a joke, but it set Richard thinking. So far everything had been based on physics and engineering, but for selecting the driver they needed to apply some psychology.

He began by setting a kind of initiative test. He called a press conference and, in the course of describing the *ThrustSSC* project, he mentioned that he wasn't going to drive the car himself. He didn't specifically say he was looking for applicants, nor did he say how anybody interested in the job could get in touch with him. After all, the future driver of a car built to go a mile in under five seconds ought to be able to figure things out for himself.

Thirty-two people got in touch. Richard was able to whittle the list down to sixteen on the basis of their experience with speed-related vehicles. All of these turned out to be either drag racers or pilots, which seemed to make sense.

Richard took his sixteen candidates to Professor Roger Green, a professor of psychology, who gave them a series of tests at

DERA in Farnborough. Professor Green began on the assumption that the driver had to possess the reflexes and courage to handle *ThrustSSC*, but on top of that he needed other qualities. He must be a person the rest of the team could get on with – not arrogant or sulky. He had to be intelligent, because his observations while testing the car would help direct the design. By the same token, he mustn't be too dominant a personality because the whole project depended on teamwork.

One of the tests lasted twenty-four hours and was designed to evaluate the candidates' ability to handle stress. And at each stage Professor Green was able to make a judgement about which candidates would go through to the next stage.

It came down to five men. The psychology tests had shown that they all might be suitable, but now it was time to put these shortlisted candidates behind the wheel of a car.

Richard took them on a bus to a rally school at Saltburn in Yorkshire. There they were introduced to rally champion Russell Brookes, who took each of them on a couple of mile-long instruction laps in an F2 Volkswagen Golf rally car. After this, they were told, each could do two quicker laps at their own pace to get a feel for the vehicle. After that they must do three high-speed laps with no instruction from Russell.

'If you spin off during the four practice laps it doesn't matter,' Richard told them. 'The final three laps are a different matter, though. We'll have the clocks running, there can only be one winner, and anyone who spins is out.'

> 'The idea behind the rally test wasn't to equate the ability to drive a rally car with the ability to handle a supersonic car. The latter doesn't go round a track, for one thing. OK, some of it was a test of reflexes, but all these people were pilots in any case.
>
> 'No, what we were really looking at was the ability to cope in an unfamiliar situation. It could just as easily have been speedboats. What mattered was how the candidates learned and adapted.'
>
> — RICHARD NOBLE

It fell to Dick Downs, a 32-year-old RAF Tornado pilot, to set the ball rolling. He got up too much speed before braking at the approach to a tight bend. The car fishtailed violently, and went into a ditch.

Downs waited while the car was hauled out. To his credit, the mishap didn't upset him at all. He simply wanted to use his free laps to discover his limit, so he would know what he was doing on the timed laps. Ironically, although he had learned from his mistake, it was to cause one of the other applicants to fail.

Downs finished his remaining laps without incident and was followed by Andy Green and Bernie Smith, both also Tornado pilots, and commercial pilots Steve Warren-Smith and David Ramsden.

It was Bernie Smith who went awry because of Downs's run. None of them got to see each other's laps, of course, so after the long hold-up he assumed that Downs must have been knocked out of the running for a mishap during his timed laps. Reasoning that he now only had three rivals to worry about instead of four, Smith let caution be his watchword and netted a time of 4 minutes 51 seconds. Warren-Smith placed fourth on 4 minutes 48.036 seconds and

Ramsden third on 4 minutes 47.576 seconds.

It was a close-run thing because Downs and Green came in with best lap times of 4 minutes 33 seconds and 4 minutes 34 seconds respectively.

Despite their very close times, Dick Downs and Andy Green had differed greatly in their approach. Downs went hell-for-leather regardless of spinning off early on, whereas Andy Green took things one step at a time and got progressively faster with each lap.

Andy Green's comments after the rally runs were illuminating. 'I was looking at each lap and trying to go quicker each time,' he said. 'But I wasn't necessarily going for the fastest time because I knew that Richard was looking at the results from a whole battery of tests, not just these rally results.'

It was beginning to look like Andy because he showed the steadiness and ability to learn. But all of them were top-notch people and there was one more test remaining. Could they work in the team?

The last test had an element of trickery. Each candidate was told that he would be assessed on a written report on the entire project, evaluating its chances of success and designing the instrument panel. They didn't know it was a ruse – and nor did the team, with whom they had to spend a great deal of time in order to evaluate the project. It was just a device to get each of the candidates to meet each of the existing team members. It worked terribly well. When the reports had been written, Richard and Ron activated the next stage, which involved a special questionnaire designed by Professor Green being sent to the entire *ThrustSSC* team and, from the results that he got back, Professor Green was able to establish that Andy Green was the man they felt would be the best team person.

On 2 February 1995 it was announced that Squadron Leader Andy Green would be the driver to take *ThrustSSC* through the sound barrier.

Richard said later: 'The crucial thing was there was no selection by a panel, no subjective element. We didn't select Andy – he won the competition. Professor Green simply made his judgement on points based on performance in the tests, and objectively Andy came out on top. We wanted to be sure of getting the best man, and the way to do that was to go about it scientifically. History proves we were right.'

'I was just finishing at university when Richard Noble took the land speed record in Thrust2. I was about to begin officer training with the RAF back then, and what he'd done inspired me tremendously.

'When I saw the news about the press launch for the ThrustSSC project, there was just one line in the article that said, "Richard won't be driving the car this time; he's looking for someone else."

'Now I thought to myself, who on earth would you find to drive a supersonic car? What sort of qualifications would they need? The more I thought about it, the more it seemed those qualifications would be those of a jet pilot rather than a racing driver. I suddenly decided, OK, if they need a jet pilot, who is better qualified to drive that car than me? Nobody. Right, it's got to be my job, then. And I wrote a letter to Richard that afternoon.'

— ANDY GREEN, *ThrustSSC driver*

TWELVE

Craig Breedlove was a very serious contender for the supersonic land speed record. The new *Spirit of America* car he was building was *ThrustSSC*'s rival.

Breedlove had been a major world figure in the land speed record field for thirty years. Even now, in his sixties, he ran three miles every day. Richard took to joking that Breedlove must have the secret of eternal youth, and perhaps he did. The secret is enthusiasm, and Breedlove tackled everything in his life with boundless enthusiasm.

He had been the first man to go through 600 m.p.h. on land in his *Spirit of America Sonic 1* vehicle, way back in 1965. Three years earlier, with his original *Spirit of America* jet car, he had lost his braking parachute at 400 m.p.h. and melted the wheel brakes before crashing into a brine lake, having demolished a telegraph pole on the way. Breedlove swam ashore and stood laughing with relief; 'For my next trick,' he said, 'I'll set myself on fire.'

Breedlove's design was a slim pencil-shape with front wheels very close together, rear wheels outrigged and sheathed in streamlined spats. It had a single General Motors J79 8 series afterburning turbojet giving 88,000 newtons of thrust. The overall length was to be 14 metres and it had an estimated weight of 4 tonnes. Breedlove planned to sit right in the front of the circular fuselage, just in front of the front wheels and engine.

To the amazement of Richard and the *Thrust* team, Breedlove decided against wind tunnel testing. 'I'm just designing it by eye,' he told people. 'I did consider rocket sled testing like Richard Noble tried in Britain, but it's expensive.'

The new car would be called *Spirit of America*. It was to have several unusual features. The aluminium wheels were shod with filament-wound composite, like solid tyres. And where

ThrustSSC used carbon disc brakes, Breedlove did away with wheel brakes altogether. Instead he had a ski brake that would press down into the ground. He called it his Fred Flintstone brake.

In a way, from the sponsors' point of view the best thing would be for *ThrustSSC* and the *Spirit of America* to be completed at the same time. Then there'd be every chance of a 'Great Race' that would attract the maximum publicity. But the truth was, that was unlikely to happen. At this stage, the Great Race was between the two workshops, one in Britain and the other in America, to be first to construct their supersonic car.

THE GREAT RACE

'There were two teams working on supersonic cars: ourselves and Craig Breedlove's crew. It wasn't likely that we'd both complete the work simultaneously. It was likely that one team would get there first, and that would knock the other one out of the running.

'In financial terms it meant that if you had debts and then your rival went supersonic, you would go bust. Once someone had already gone supersonic

> *there would be no more sponsorship money.*
>
> *'Even worse than that, with ThrustSSC we were building a twin-engined car with quite a radical design. We had a lot of data to check. We discovered that ThrustSSC would take 100,000 man hours to build, while Breedlove's simpler car might need 20,000 man hours. So it was a simple if harrowing equation – for every man-hour Craig's team put in, we had to do five.'*
>
> — RICHARD NOBLE

Nor was Breedlove *Thrust*'s only rival. Another contender was about to emerge. During the earlier research phase, Richard had heard rumours about the McLaren Formula One team, how they were interested in the prestige to be won in a land speed record project.

One day Richard had got a call from McLaren asking for video of *Thrust2*. He deliberately stalled to see if they'd call again, and they did. At the same time he heard from various friends throughout the industry about McLaren designers who were researching data on the land speed record.

There couldn't be any doubt. McLaren were

planning a land speed project of their own.

Obviously with McLaren's resources there would be no problem with raising finance. They had the resources to undertake a very big and expensive project and effectively buy the land speed record. The news might have been disastrous for the *Thrust* team's morale, but in fact it had the opposite effect. The *Thrust* team was determined that McLaren wouldn't take the supersonic record without a terrific fight.

The McLaren car design was unveiled at a press conference. It was to be called the *Maverick*. It would be 15 metres long, weigh a little over 3 tonnes, and be powered by a Rolls-Royce RB199 engine. None of these ideas was very revolutionary in itself, but where McLaren would be breaking fresh ground was in the use of carbon fibre composites for the chassis. Like *ThrustSSC*, the *Maverick* would also have a computer-controlled active suspension system – one that could alter the pitch of the car in motion to control aerodynamic lift.

There was intense speculation in the media as to who would drive the *Maverick*. Many people thought this was Ayrton Senna's car. Even though Senna had left McLaren in 1993, the company's managing director insisted, 'Ayrton will one day drive for McLaren again.'

Was Senna really down to drive the *Maverick*? Tragically we will never know, for he was killed at Imola on 1 May 1994.

Ron Ayers reassured everyone on the *ThrustSSC* team that McLaren would eventually have to halt their Maverick project. 'The only way you can build a supersonic car with adequate stability is with a twin-engine arrangement,' he argued. 'McLaren's trouble is, if they've done the CFD analysis, they'll know they need rocket sled testing as well, and that takes time. For reasons of stability, they might well realize that they need two engines and they'll have to decide what to do – whether to press on with the design they've got and hope for the best, or switch to something more like our design. In that case it will look like they're copying *ThrustSSC* and their sponsors won't be so keen.'

Time went by and there was silence from the McLaren camp. By the end of 1996 it was clear they had quietly allowed the *Maverick* project to lapse.

ThrustSSC's only supersonic opponent was Craig Breedlove's *Spirit of America*.

THIRTEEN

It was about this time that Richard began to realize that *ThrustSSC* was outgrowing its workshop. Work had started at the G-Force premises in Fontwell in June 1994. But by now *ThrustSSC* had grown so large that it was taking up the whole of the G-Force assembly hall – and the team were falling over each other as they tried to work on it. Priceless time was being wasted – the moment had come when *ThrustSSC* had to be moved to a much larger workshop – and preferably one with an aircraft runway at the door for low speed testing.

Fortunately at the same time, Andy Green was transferred to DERA at Farnborough. He made some enquiries and they enthusiastically offered Richard the use of Q Shed, a huge green hangar.

This was a great opportunity. Farnborough has a long runway and *ThrustSSC* could only benefit from the expertise on hand at DERA. And their luck didn't end there. Andy's main responsibility involved the JOUST air combat simulator. It was relatively easy, using Ron's very detailed data, to create a driver simulator for *ThrustSSC*. Even though the real car had yet to turn its wheels, by the end of 1995 Andy was able to get a feel for how it would be to drive the world's fastest land vehicle.

'When I drove the ThrustSSC simulator for the first time, it was awesome. I couldn't believe how fast it accelerated — and I wasn't even using the after-burner.

'That first time it got way ahead of me, but with a simulator like this, you practise a few times and you see you've got to watch this, this and this. So you begin to catch up.

'Overtraining on a simulator is bad because you can end up training for the simulation rather than the reality. But this was useful for giving me some idea of what to expect.

'We also used the simulator for research. Ron Ayers was running all the datasheets on the perfor-mance of the car itself, and we could crosscheck that with the simulator. It was the same data, but we were testing it on two very different computer programs and getting the same results, which was very encouraging.'

— ANDY GREEN

*

As 1995 rolled into 1996, *ThrustSSC* began to show real progress. The Spey engines had already been tested at Shoeburyness, where they had roared their awesome power at the Proof and Experimental Establishment. Now, in July 1996, they were fitted onto the car and the whole car was taken to Boscombe Down for the first static test.

ThrustSSC was tethered in place and Andy climbed aboard. It was a breathless moment for Richard and everyone else on the team. Richard in particular was struck by how far things had come from his early days with *Thrust1* in 1975. *ThrustSSC* was three times the size and had twelve times the power of *Thrust1*.

Andy fired up the engines. 'The sight of *ThrustSSC* sitting there with each engine in turn blasting out virtually 100,000 newtons of thrust was simply spellbinding,' remembers Richard. 'It was the day that I knew for sure we were going to do it, we were going to win.'

*

> *'It was really only when the team was getting ready to go to Jordan that I began to think it would actually happen. I'd seen it being built but it wasn't very impressive then. It was all in bits – bits of scaffolding. But when we started to do the engine tests, that was good. We did a lot of runs at Farnborough. I had to stay in Dad's car because of the safety rules at Farnborough, but I would stand and watch out of the sun roof and watch it tearing down the runway at 200 m.p.h. In between the runs, I listened to the radio, the walkie-talkies.'*
>
> — *JACK NOBLE: Richard Noble's son*

DERA, Farnborough, and Boscombe Down were fine for static tests and short low-speed runs, but to put *ThrustSSC* through its paces they would need a much longer course. There was nowhere suitable in the U.K and the age-old problem with the desert sites in America was the short dry season. If you missed that opportunity you would have to wait for a year for the desert to get dry again.

To pull ahead of Craig Breedlove, they needed to get in as many test runs as possible. Richard's brother, Andrew, had been scouring the world for other suitable desert locations.

Now he got a report from someone who had been stationed near the al Jafr Desert, in Jordan in 1950. 'I have never forgotten driving across the al Jafr mud flats,' wrote the man. 'It was as smooth and flat as a billiards table. I'd just set the throttle, put my feet up, and away I'd go. It felt like I was floating.'

Richard made some enquiries. Prince Faisal al Hussein was very happy for them to come over to Jordan. He would see to it that they could rent everything they needed – a military base to operate out of, accommodation for the whole crew, a hangar to work on the car. The weather was outside his control, but it hadn't rained in Jordan for five years so the desert was perfect right now.

Richard's aim was to get *ThrustSSC* up to 600 m.p.h. in Jordan before heading back home and preparing for America. He worked out that they had almost a hundred tonnes of gear to transport. There was not just *ThrustSSC* but also its trailer and truck, the Pit Station (the communications, Internet and computing nerve centre) and its tractor unit, two Supacats to tow *ThrustSSC* into position, the Merlo forklift truck for engine changes, and the famous Kidde Jaguar Firechase.

They couldn't afford to waste precious weeks at sea and the team had only a few days to get to Jordan. The whole lot, 100 tonnes, was loaded aboard an enormous HeavyLift Antonov 124 freighter and flown out.

Barely had they arrived at the King Faisal Air Base than news came from Black Rock. Craig Breedlove had survived a horrendous accident at 675 m.p.h. It appeared that a supersonic shockwave had developed under his car, which had then rolled onto its side and raced violently around in a huge two-mile circle. By some miracle, nobody had been injured, though apparently a camper had been parked on the scene of the accident only an hour before, moving on by lucky chance just before the run commenced. By sheer good fortune Craig was unhurt, but *Spirit of America* had been severely damaged.

Clearly the new car had potential. It had the power, but did it have the stability? Breedlove's accident suggested not, although he claimed the cause of the crash was a freak sidewind that had lifted the rear wheels. Either way, he had to go back to the workshop with a damaged car and it would be a year before he could challenge Richard's land speed record again.

The first task before the testing of *ThrustSSC* could begin was the defodding of the desert. This was necessary because of all the loose stones on the desert which could easily be hoovered into *ThrustSSC*'s engine intakes. Defodding the course in Jordan involved teams of people walking abreast along the course, getting down on their knees gouging out stones with screwdrivers. A two hundred and eighty kilometre stretch of desert had to be scoured clean. 'It's like clearing the A303 from Hyde Park Corner to Exeter!' Ron explained.

Early runs soon saw *ThrustSSC* to 325 m.p.h., despite the car taking an impact loading of twenty tonnes as it crossed a track through the desert. These tracks were made by Bedouin crossing the desert in heavy trucks. When Andy hit one of these ruts at speed, the wheels would leave the ground for twenty-five metres or more.

Jeremy Bliss, who had designed the vehicle systems including the very clever active suspension, made some adjustments to soften the impacts but even so they had to go carefully.

'There's no way we'll get a land speed record on this surface,' Ron said. 'We don't have enough run-off at the ends of the course, for one thing. All we can do is get the data, fix each problem as we spot it, and keep improving the speeds.'

The idea had been to come to Jordan and stay as long as they needed to in order to get *ThrustSSC* to 600 m.p.h. They had a lot of food, plenty of supplies and spares, and everyone was determined to sit it out come hell or high water.

The high water wasn't long in coming. After only five weeks in Jordan, and having achieved only 340 m.p.h. with *ThrustSSC*, it started to pour with rain. By 27 November much of the painstakingly defodded course was flooded. Richard had no choice. He gave the order to pack up and head home.

It was a bad moment – perhaps the bleakest in *ThrustSSC*'s long development time. The trip to Jordan had been a failure, the finances were stretched almost beyond endurance, morale was at its lowest ebb.

What got them through the next stage was the Mach One Club.

The Mach One Club had been started by Robin Richardson, a lifelong enthusiast for record-breaking whom Richard had known for years. Many of the Mach One Club's members were veterans from the old *Thrust2* Supporters' Club, but just as many were newcomers. The club had grown over the course of the project and now had a paid-up membership of over four thousand.

Weekend after weekend, the Mach One Club members would turn out in force at the *ThrustSSC* open days at Farnborough. Richard explained the situation to them, honestly and without embellishment, and they appreciated that the project was going through an appalling financial crisis. There would be auctions to sell off life-expired parts of the car, and huge volumes of T-shirts and other merchandise were sold. The club members dug deep in their pockets. By the end of the project, Richard was later to comment, their contributions accounted for twenty per cent of the entire budget and made the Mach One Club the largest sponsor.

By the spring, with money from BTR plc, the team had rebuilt *ThrustSSC* and were keen to get back to Jordan. They had one last chance to get the car ready before the autumn season in Black Rock. If this trip didn't pay off, it would spell the end for *ThrustSSC*, because no sponsor would stick with it for another whole year.

Richard managed to raise just enough to pay

for the flight out. 'Our backs are to the wall,' he told everyone, 'and this time there's no coming back without a good result. There will be no more money and if we do badly we'll just have to break up *ThrustSSC* for scrap to pay the bills. So let's make this one count!'

Perhaps it was Richard's pep talk, perhaps it was the experience they'd gained the first time, but from the day they arrived in Jordan for the second time, the team bonded well and they produced startling results.

Within two weeks they had hit speeds of 540 m.p.h. There had been some minor delays from the intense heat affecting the electronics and computers, but then a rear suspension bracket failure after several severe impacts on the uneven desert terminated further running.

Returning from Jordan for the second time saw them all in a very different mood. The team had done well and they knew that they had a good chance of taking *ThrustSSC* supersonic.

One thing remained. The moment of truth. All they had worked for would be put to the test just four months away, in Black Rock, Nevada.

FOURTEEN

'If the project had financial problems before, it was now in very serious difficulties. The problem was that to pay the debts, to fund the project for five weeks and to fund the cost of going to America was going to need £600,000. And we had only about two months in which to make that money. We had a very generous offer from HeavyLift, the company that had flown us to Jordan, to help out with moving everything over to America. But we still had to pay for the aeroplane fuel. It was about £140,000 for that fuel alone, never mind all our other costs, and at first I couldn't see how we could raise it. We approached all the major oil companies and they all turned us down. How on earth were we going to fund the trip?

'The answer was to use the Internet. Our website had got ten million hits already, so we put up a piece explaining that this was our last chance. We were asking people all over the world to buy our fuel for us. In return they would get a fuel certificate signed by Andy. Overnight, people from over a hundred different countries started buying thirty thousand gallons of fuel a day!

'Then the Daily Telegraph ran a series of features about the project and asked the question why it was that we were unable to raise enough money to go to America. The readers responded by sending us money – £15,000 a day. Putting together the money we had made already, the fuel money, and the Daily Telegraph readers' money, we were just a little short of the budget and I was able to borrow the rest from Castrol.

'We left to go to America three days late.'

– RICHARD NOBLE

Getting started on the Black Rock course was, as usual, a matter of building up the speeds in small stages. It was a new desert and new conditions.

The runs began on 8 September 1997 and the

first time was a leisurely 148 m.p.h., to check the car out. By stages, Andy took the car up to 500 m.p.h. By the eleventh run the speed peaked at 624 m.p.h., and Andy said that even then he was 'just loafing along'.

Glynne Bowsher was particularly pleased with the way the car was performing, after the pounding it had taken at al Jafr. 'The Black Rock playa doesn't have those undulations and isn't as hard as the al Jafr desert. Here, *ThrustSSC* has all four wheels on the ground at all speeds. In Jordan there were times when none of them were in contact with the ground!'

'When we were in the desert, I used to fax my school reports of how it was going, and everybody in the class wrote a letter back. I had maths sheets, sums, angles, spelling to do, but not real lessons. One day we were coming into the desert for one of the major runs and the sheriff came up to me and said, 'Why's that kid not in school?'

'Mum said, "Because his name's Noble!"

'He laughed and said, "Right!"'

— JACK NOBLE: *Richard Noble's son*

But just as one aspect of the car – the mechanical engineering – was really coming together, another threatened to waste precious days. This time it was the computers. There were two onboard computers, both fairly antiquated. *Comp One* dealt with all the safety systems and therefore would shut the car down if it sensed anything it didn't like. *Comp Two* handled data acquisition and kept an eye on *Comp One*.

Now, in two successive runs, *Comp One* had initiated an automatic shut-down. It happened at the exact same spot in both runs. The worrying thing was whether there was some major hidden fault, or whether the computer itself was acting up.

'If that computer has started seeing things,' said Jeremy, the Systems Designer, 'we are totally stuffed.'

Had *ThrustSSC* become a victim of its own hi-tech design? The base cost of staying at Black Rock was $5000 a day, whether the car ran or not, so it was vital to identify the trouble fast.

They knew that the playa surface was damaging to delicate machinery. 'You only had to leave a window open a fraction and everything would be coated in a layer of dust like talcum powder,' recalls Richard. '*ThrustSSC* was whipping up clouds of the stuff. Worse still it was an alkaline dust that would start to corrode metal components.'

Luckily the problem turned out to be simply a computer connection. Jeremy rectified the fault and, by the third week of September, Richard had called in the USAC timekeepers. Dave Petrali and the USAC team had timed the *Thrust2* record in 1983. If Richard's team were going to achieve the sound barrier with *ThrustSSC*, it was essential that the attempt was properly timed, observed and accredited.

On Thursday 25 September there had been a light rain falling since dawn, but it didn't seem to have affected the twenty-five kilometre course at all. Andy made a first run at just a shade over 700 m.p.h. Richard waited at the midpoint with the media for the car to be turned around and sent back. Then he saw it, thundering across the desert, a shimmering black arrow tearing up its own white dust storm.

Jayne Millington, the Runs Controller announced, '*ThrustSSC* is safe, safe, safe.' Then came the news from the USAC timekeeper: 'Speed through the mile: 728.081 m.p.h.' The two runs were to average 714.144 m.p.h. – not only a new World Record but also the largest jump in the land speed record ever – over eighty miles per hour faster!

Richard realized he'd been holding his breath and let it out with a sigh. Everyone around him was exploding into screams of delight. His own feelings ran much deeper than simple triumph. He had just watched another man beat his own world record – something which would have been heartbreaking, perhaps, except that it was in the car which Richard himself had master-minded.

'When the moment came, I knew I'd willingly trade my own personal record for being a part of the best team ever. These weren't the old days of Sir Henry Segrave and Sir Malcolm Campbell, where the boss was also the driver. The only way we could have done ThrustSSC was how we did: through teamwork. That means the very best person for each job. In the case of the driver that meant Andy Green, and I'd been working day and night for six years to make sure he took my record away from me.'

– RICHARD NOBLE

Meanwhile, what of Craig Breedlove? If *ThrustSSC* had suffered from bad luck, it was nothing to the trouble Breedlove had had. First his engine had sucked in bolts from a wheel change and the engine had to be stripped down and changed. Then had come a problem with the afterburner, which was holding him back from reaching higher speeds. Added to all this, he had just as much difficulty as Richard in finding sponsorship. So at this point he was lagging behind in the race, leaving the *ThrustSSC* team with a clear field.

Then, at the eleventh hour and with victory in sight, a huge row blew up that almost split the team apart.

THE ACTIVE SUSPENSION

The active suspension altered the pitch of the car – the relative height fore and aft – to take account of the changes in the car's aerodynamics at different speeds. Very early on it was decided not to make the active suspension a closed system. This meant that it didn't simply monitor the load on the front suspension and vary the load to keep that load within specified parameters. The runs had shown the front wheel loads initially rising with speed increase and then falling, and all highly predictable. So an 'attitude profile' for the car against speed was programmed into the computer which maintained the front wheel loads within the required limits.

Five layers of fail-safe logic circuitry ensured that no component or system failure could result in the car becoming airborne. A sophisticated abort system ensured that, if the front wheels of the car started to lift from the ground, the active suspension would tilt the nose low, giving a sudden aerodynamic download.

What had happened was that several of the design team had insisted on locking the active suspension. They were concerned that in certain circumstances the active suspension might drop the rear end of the car before jacking it up. In the split-second that took, they thought, *ThrustSSC* would start to fly.

Jeremy Bliss disagreed strongly. He had designed and programmed the active suspension to avoid any such thing. And with the active suspension disabled, there was no allowance for aerodynamics and the car could not be adjusted for aerodynamic loads and that would hold the car back. In a way, it was his competence and his entire contribution to the project which were being challenged.

It seemed like an impasse and there were rows behind the scenes. Two runs with the active suspension locked in the full down position had to be aborted due to instability before the engineering team took the decision to reinstate the active suspension. Eventually they reached a compromise. The hydraulic 'abort' element of each strut would be mechanically locked at full height in order to raise the 'minimum' height of the rear of the car, whilst reinstating the active suspension with shorter struts in order to limit the 'maximum' height. Now the active suspension could not lower the rear of the car to the critical pitch angle that would cause 'take off'.

ThrustSSC was back in action again on 6 October. The day began with a run by Craig Breedlove, who was still having trouble with his afterburner. He achieved a speed of 531 m.p.h.

Then it was Andy's turn. He finished his run a whisker under Mach 0.97. A stripped bolt prevented the return run, but it was a minor fault, easily fixed. The important thing was they had proved the new suspension set-up was working.

'We had two Pegasus microlights so that we could check that the course was clear. One day, Simon Baker took me up with him so that I could watch Spirit of America run. We took off but we had to come into land quickly because there was something wrong with the seat and then, when we came back up again, there was just dust. We had missed the run! I never saw Spirit of America run. The first time I was there to watch it, I was busy getting deckchairs and, by the time I got back, it was just dust. He'd already done it.

'The microlight goes up very quickly. They just push forward on the bar connected to the wings. It's quite scary because there's the propeller right behind you. I had headphones on to talk to the pilot, or to the bus, Mum's merchandise vehicle.

'Mum's bus had loads of ThrustSSC merchandise like T-shirts, hats and other stuff in it. In the desert

One of the microlight pilots who had flown
over the desert reported having seen a shockwave extending from the sides of the car. It was
the first sign of the supersonic shockwave.

'It's rare to actually see a shockwave except in
humid conditions, which we certainly don't
have here,' remarked Ron. 'But if one is
developing under the car it could suck up
dust, which may have given the flow visual-
isation the pilot saw.'

Someone asked Andy. 'How stable was the
track?'

Andy grinned. 'The track was completely
stable. It hasn't moved all day.'

Everyone laughed. They had cleared the air,
regained their sense of humour. Like mountain-
eers roped together, they had slipped but now
they were climbing again. And they had the
summit in sight.

FIFTEEN

'On 12 October we cleared the desert and had a private run. I believe we went supersonic then but there was no official timing that day.

'On Monday 13 October, we tried for the super-sonic record but because the afterburner flames burned the parachutes, Andy overran the course by one and a half miles and we made the return run forty-six seconds too late.

'And then came the morning of Wednesday 15 October.'

— RICHARD NOBLE

Richard had been up since five o'clock. Out on the desert, after the pre-run briefing, there was just one thing to say:

'Today we want two runs averaging Mach 1.01 at the very least. That will mean we've finally done it and we can all go home!'

Richard pretended to cover a yawn as if it was all just routine by now, but he could feel the buzz of excitement in the team. The truth was, it was now or never. The car was going to be due for a complete overhaul within the next few runs. If they didn't clock up the speed they needed by then, it would mean another week in the workshop. There was that inexorable five thousand dollars' operating cost every day, and the project had long since gone over the brink financially.

Richard was asked later if he'd ever thought of calling it off. 'Because of the money? Never,' he said. 'It was once in a lifetime. I couldn't blow it just because I was worried about the debts. I'd have regretted that for the rest of my life.'

The onlookers crowded into the Press Pen, Richard among them. To his annoyance, he found himself thinking of the rocket sled tests, when the *ThrustSSC* model had exploded into a million pieces. It was a horribly graphic reminder of what could happen if things went wrong. He had seen the static tests, too, where the shockwaves in the engine afterburner flames buffetted the rear fuselage of *ThrustSSC*, rippling the thick titanium skin.

Attention to safety had of course been a priority all through the project, and that was the way to minimize risk. *ThrustSSC* took a severe beating every run, largely because of the tremendous sound and heat damage from the engines, together with the alkaline dust in the machinery. When he had flown over the desert a few days earlier, Richard had been appalled to see how *ThrustSSC*'s tracks, which from the ground had looked dead straight, were in fact wavering all over the place. That was when he understood what a hard job it had been for Andy just to keep the car on the course.

Craig Breedlove came in to join them at their moment of triumph. It must have been a disappointing time for him, but he had enjoyed his triumphs in the past. He sportingly acknowledged that this was Andy's day.

The minutes ticked round to 9:00 a.m. and the countdown began. At eight minutes past, Jayne

Millington, the Runs Controller, announced that *ThrustSSC* was rolling. There it came, rocketing down the desert in complete silence, outrunning the sound of its own engine.

ThrustSSC raced past, the dust rising like a thundercloud behind it. It became a molten shimmer in the morning sunlight, a mirage in the immensity of the desert.

And then it came. The roar of air being split apart at the speed of sound. The double sonic boom that told them *ThrustSSC* had done it.

It was the sound that made history.

Twelve miles away, in the town of Gerlach, Nevada, it was as if a miniature earthquake had hit. Pictures shook off walls, plates flew from dressers. The sprinkler caps shook loose in the school classrooms and the thunderous double boom gave everyone a huge shock.

In the Press Pen there was such a commotion that Richard had trouble hearing the time-keeper's official speed.

It was 759.333 m.p.h. – Mach 1.016. The team had the first of the two supersonic record runs in the bag!

'When ThrustSSC is travelling at supersonic speeds it is a truly spectacular sight. Imagine you are standing on Black Rock Desert with all the television and press reporters and camera crews. It is still early in the morning, the best time to run, and the air temperature is still very cold – even though this is a desert. The excitement and anticipation are intense. From a nearby handheld radio you hear the ThrustSSC ground crew talking with each other and checking that the car is ready to run and all team members are in position. Overhead a microlight spotter place checks that the desert is clear, and no-one is travelling across it. The radio crackles "SSC is rolling".

'The first thing you see in the distance is a dust cloud. It gradually gets closer until the car itself becomes visible as a small shimmering spot moving ever faster across the horizon. The dust cloud is enormous, spreading to a height of several hundreds of feet. Curiously, you cannot hear the car. How can an enormous car with two jet engines producing 100,000 horsepower be totally silent? Then it occurs to you. As the car is travelling faster than the speed of sound, the noise it is creating cannot get ahead of it. You will only be able to hear *it when it has already gone past.*

'Suddenly the car seems quite close. It is travelling very fast indeed, taking just 4¾ seconds to travel one mile. As ThrustSSC passes in front of you, all the noise that could not reach you before arrives together, and combined with the shockwave produced by the supersonic flow around the car, it creates an enormous noise like an explosion. It is such a deep 'boom' that it shakes your chest and stomach as well as your ears. The roar of the engines continues as ThrustSSC disappears again over the horizon. All around there is great excitement, and some anxiety as everyone awaits the all-important radio message that "ThrustSSC is safe". The dust cloud is now drifting in your direction, blotting out the sun and if you don't move you will soon be covered by a layer of fine dust.'

– RON AYERS: Chief Aerodynamicist

The other team members with Richard were almost screaming with elation and relief, but he just gritted his teeth. 'We need another run within the hour to make it a record.'

ThrustSSC was turned around, towed into position and prepared for the return run. It took almost an hour – an agonizing wait, but everyone was too tense to speak. There would be just a few words of conversation now and then, soon lapsing into silence. Then Jayne's voice came over the radio: '*SSC* rolling. Clear supersonic.' It was four minutes after ten.

ThrustSSC whipcracked by, bringing its storm of desert dust behind it. Both runs had been within the hour, and Richard held his breath as he waited to hear the timekeeper's announcement.

'Speed through the mile: 766.609 miles an hour.' After an agony of delay, the timekeeper added, '*SSC*, your Mach number was 1.02.'

Success!

The world's first supersonic land speed record had been set at 763.035 m.p.h.

Richard hugged his wife, shook hands with all the team, then went out to answer the media's questions.

'How does it feel?' somebody asked him.

Richard let out a long sigh. 'We really did it! Thank God it's over.'

'I got up from my bed before daylight and went to breakfast. Breakfast was served at the Community Centre by two huge ladies, Bonnie and Lola. I had cereal and milk and after that, sausages and eggs. I got into Mum's merchandise wagon (an old school bus) with her and set off for the desert. We had a very bumpy ride to the desert because there are so many holes in the ground. On the way down, there was a diversion on the road, so we had to drive off the road and drive on very bumpy desert mud all the way there.

'When we got to the Pit Station, Dad and I led millions of journalists to the Press Pen in the measured mile (which is in the middle of the track). After that, we had to take the car keys away from the press in case they wanted a good photo and drove after ThrustSSC. After the team had taken the keys away from the press, they radioed through to the Pit Station to say that they were ready. Then SSC Radio called to see if the track was clear to roll the car. But Pit Station said "No!" because there was a bandit (an intruder) on the track. So the SSC Security came into action after the bandit, the bandit stopped and the SSC Security came and led him off the desert. Then the Pit Station came through to say the track was now clear so the SSC could roll. So the car began to roll very slowly, then got faster and faster until it was zooming through the measured mile completely silent until . . .

BOOM BOOM!

'The car was now roaring like Concorde again, then the 'chutes were fired and the car drifted across the desert like a boat on the sea. The next thing I heard was "Pit Station, this is USAC timing," and saying the speed. We knew the car had gone supersonic. Now the next mission was to get the car back within the hour. Then the car was given permission to roll again. There was a kick of dust at the end of the track that told us the car had started its engines. Then the car started to roll, it drifted for a second and then it started to accelerate, it came past in complete silence then . . .

BOOM BOOM!

'Then the 'chutes were fired and the car started to decrease its speed. Then it stopped and that was the end of our mission. Party-time!'

– JACK NOBLE: Richard Noble's son

The party in Gerlach lasted all afternoon and evening. Andy Green – with Jayne riding pillion – rode his motorcycle straight into the

Black Rock Saloon, in the door and right up to the bar. He had worked hard, now he felt entitled to play hard.

But before letting his hair down at the party, he had diligently filed one last driver's report. Part of it read, *'Subjective feeling that rear-wheel steering should be limited to forklift trucks in future.'*

And there wasn't a man in the world better qualified to express such an opinion.

'People asked why we didn't go for 800 m.p.h. Our aim was to set a two-way average above Mach One and we did it. The big surprise was we were getting near the car's performance limit. We thought it could go on comfortably up to 850 m.p.h., but in practice we were hitting a wall at Mach One. The drag was shooting up just when it should have been dropping.

'We don't yet know why this was. It may have been that the transonic drag rise hadn't reached its peak. Possibly you need to get to Mach 1.3 or so before a uniform supersonic flow is established over the whole vehicle surface.

'Also, the transonic ground effect was pummelling the surface under the car. Effectively, instead of four separate wheel tracks we were ploughing a twelve-foot furrow across the playa.

> *Churning up twelve feet of baked mud at 771 m.p.h. takes an enormous amount of energy.*
>
> *'Six months later, we're still investigating all the data. ThrustSSC wasn't just about that one day in the desert. It was an experimental project which gained data which will be useful to generations of land speed record breakers to come.'*
>
> — RICHARD NOBLE

Summing up his feelings about the project later, Richard said, 'I don't believe in fate. My philosophy is that you earn your own luck. You can't just expect it – teddy bears in the cockpit, lucky charms, they're useless. You have to work hard and earn it.

'You only get one spell on this wonderful planet. It's up to you to make the best of it. If it benefits other people as well, then so much the better. It's a hard grind and you can't expect anything other than that. Why should you? You shouldn't lead yourself, or anyone else for that matter, to expect that you are going to get an easy ride. It doesn't happen that way. Lunches never come free.

You make your own progress and your own luck. By determination, commitment, refusal to give up or be straightjacketed by convention or the short-sightedness of others – describe it as you will – you are the only one who creates the airflow beneath your own wings.

THRUSTSSC

Records and Achievements ratified by FIA

World Land Speed Record
25 September 1997
Mile: 714.144 m.p.h. (1149.272 k.p.h.)
Kilo: 713.990 m.p.h. (1149.024 k.p.h.)

First ever ratified supersonic run
13 October 1997
Mach No: 1.006

Supersonic Land Speed Record
15 October 1997
Mile: 763.035 m.p.h. (1227.952 k.p.h.)
Kilo: 760.343 m.p.h. (1223.620 k.p.h.)
Mach No: 1.0175

From on-board data
Highest Speed Achieved: 771 m.p.h.
Highest Mach No achieved: Mach 1.030

The Land Speed Record 1898–1997

DATE	DRIVER	SPEED (M.P.H.)	CAR	VENUE
18.12.98	Gaston de Chasseloup-Laubat	39.24	Jeantaud	Acheres
17.01.99	Camille Jenatzy	41.42	Jenatzy	Acheres
17.01.99	Gaston de Chasseloup-Laubat	43.69	Jeantaud	Acheres
27.01.99	Camille Jenatzy	49.92	Jenatzy	Acheres
04.03.99	Gaston de Chasseloup-Laubat	57.60	Jeantaud	Acheres
29.04.99	Camille Jenatzy	65.79	Jenatzy	Acheres
13.04.02	Leon Serpollet	75.06	Serpollet	Nice
05.08.02	William K. Vanderbilt	76.08	Mors	Ablis
05.11.02	Henri Fournier	76.60	Mors	Dourdan
17.11.02	Augieres	77.13	Mors	Dourdan
17.07.03	Arthur Duray	83.47	Gobron-Brillie	Ostend
05.11.03	Arthur Duray	84.73	Gobron-Brillie	Dourdan
12.01.04	Henry Ford	91.37*	Ford Arrow	Lake St Clair
27.01.04	William K. Vanderbilt	92.30*	Mercedes	Daytona
31.03.04	Louis Rigolly	94.78	Gobron-Brillie	Nice

Date	Driver	Car	Speed	Location
25.05.04	Pierre de Caters	Mercedes	97.25	Ostend
21.07.04	Louis Rigolly	Gobron-Brillie	103.55	Ostend
13.11.04	Paul Baras	Darracq	104.52	Ostend
25.01.05	Arthur Macdonald	Napier	104.65*	Daytona
30.12.05	Victor Hemery	Darracq	109.65	Arles-Salon
23.01.06	Fred Marriott	Stanley	121.57	Daytona
08.11.09	Victor Hemery	Benz	125.95	Brooklands
16.04.10	Barney Oldfield	Benz	131.275*	Daytona
23.04.11	Bob Burman	Benz	141.37*	Daytona
24.06.14	L.G. Hornsted	Benz	124.10**	Brooklands
17.02.19	Ralph de Palma	Packard	149.875*	Daytona
27.04.20	Tommy Milton	Duesenberg	156.03*	Daytona
17.05.22	Kenelm Lee Guinness	Sunbeam	133.75	Brooklands
06.06.24	Rene Thomas	Delage	143.41	Arpajon
12.07.24	Ernest Eldridge	FIAT	146.01	Arpajon
25.09.24	Malcolm Campbell	Sunbeam	146.16	Pendine Sands
21.07.25	Malcolm Campbell	Sunbeam	150.76	Pendine Sands
16.03.26	Henry Segrave	Sunbeam	152.33	Southport Beach
27.04.26	Parry Thomas	Babs	169.30	Pendine Sands

Date	Driver	Car	Speed	Location
28.04.26	Parry Thomas	Babs	171.02	Pending Sands
04.02.27	Malcolm Campbell	Bluebird	174.883	Pendine Sands
29.03.27	Henry Segrave	Sunbeam	203.792	Daytona Beach
19.02.28	Malcolm Campbell	Bluebird	206.956	Daytona Beach
22.04.28	Ray Keech	White Triplex	207.552	Daytona Beach
11.03.29	Henry Segrave	Golden Arrow	231.446	Daytona Beach
05.02.31	Malcolm Campbell	Bluebird	246.090	Daytona Beach
24.02.32	Malcolm Campbell	Bluebird	253.970	Daytona Beach
22.02.33	Malcolm Campbell	Bluebird	272.460	Daytona Beach
07.03.35	Malcolm Campbell	Bluebird	276.820	Daytona Beach
03.09.35	Malcolm Campbell	Bluebird	301.129	Bonneville Salt Flats
19.11.37	George Eyston	Thunderbolt	312.000	Bonneville Salt Flats
27.08.38	George Eyston	Thunderbolt	345.500	Bonneville Salt Flats
15.09.38	John Cobb	Railton	350.200	Bonneville Salt Flats
16.09.38	George Eyston	Thunderbolt	357.500	Bonneville Salt Flats
23.08.39	John Cobb	Railton	369.700	Bonneville Salt Flats
16.09.47	John Cobb	Railton	394.194	Bonneville Salt Flats
05.08.63	Craig Breedlove	Spirit of America	407.450	Bonneville Salt Flats

Date	Driver	Vehicle	Speed	Location
17.07.64	Donald Campbell	Bluebird	403.100****	Lake Eyre
02.10.64	Tom Green	Wingfoot Express	413.200	Bonneville Salt Flats
05.10.64	Art Arfons	Green Monster	434.020	Bonneville Salt Flats
13.10.64	Craig Breedlove	Spirit of America	468.720	Bonneville Salt Flats
15.10.64	Craig Breedlove	Spirit of America	526.280	Bonneville Salt Flats
27.10.64	Art Arfons	Green Monster	536.710	Bonneville Salt Flats
02.11.65	Craig Breedlove	Spirit of America-Sonic 1	555.483	Bonneville Salt Flats
07.11.65	Art Arfons	Green Monster	576.553	Bonneville Salt Flats
13.11.65	Bob Summers	Goldenrod	409.277****	Bonneville Salt Flats
15.11.65	Craig Breedlove	Spirit of America Sonic 1	600.601	Bonneville Salt Flats
23.10.70	Gary Gabelich	The Blue Flame	622.407	Bonneville Salt Flats
04.10.83	**Richard Noble**	*Thrust2*	633.468	**Black Rock Desert**
25.09.97	**Andy Green**	*ThrustSSC*	714.144	**Black Rock Desert**
15.10.97	**Andy Green**	*ThrustSSC*	763.035*****	**Black Rock Desert**

* Not recognized by European Authority
** First mandatory two-way run
**** wheeldriven record (after 1963)   ***** First supersonic record (Mach 1.02)

Black Rock Desert Run Log 1997

RUN	DATE	PEAK SPEED (MPH)	MILE AVERAGE	KILOMETRE AVERAGE
39	08/09	148	0	0
40	08/09	50	0	0
41	10/09	306	0	0
42	10/09	428	0	0
43	10/09	517	0	0
44	11/09	550	0	0
45	11/09	624	600	600
46	13/09	550	0	0
47	20/09	410	0	0
48	20/09	554	553.97	553.931
49	22/09	650	618.556	634.77
50	22/09	689	687.941	689.347
51	23/09	697	693.507	696.863

52	23/09	721	719.137	721.358
53	25/09	706	700.661	697.95
54	25/09	731	728.008	730.784
55	03/10	560	389.483	374.194 (aborted)
56	03/10	628	0	0 (aborted)
57	06/10	721	714.427	720.428
58	06/10	732	727.86	730.546
59	07/10	750	0	0
60	07/10	170	0	0 (transit back to pits)
61	13/10	750	749.687	749.139
62	13/10	766	764.168	762.937
63	13/10	761	760.135	758.102
64	13/10	200	0	0 (transit back to pits)
65	15/10	763	759.333	756.742
66	15/10	771	766.609	763.718

Thrust Team Lists

Simon Chapman

George Myers

Richard Noble

Sally Noble

Mark Rasmussen

Birgit Ackroyd	Mike Hearn
John Ackroyd	Ninetta Hearn
Brian Ball	Andrew Noble
Mike Barnett	Charles Noble
Ron Benton	Richard Noble
Gordon Biles	Sally Noble
Glynne Bowsher	John Norris
David Brinn	Ken Norris
Mick Chambers	Ian Robinson
Richard Chisnell	David Tremayne
Lorraine Culkin	Trish Tremayne
Eddie Elsom	Simon Walmsley
Gordon Flux	John Watkins
John Griffiths	George Webb
Peter Hand	

ThrustSSC Team, 1997

Robert Atkinson

Ron Ayers

Rod Barker

Jeremy Bliss

Glynne Bowsher

Chris Cowell

Jeremy Davey

Martyn Davidson

Nick Dove

Eddie Elsom

Jack Franck

Andy Green

Mike Hearn

Ninetta Hearn

Rob Hemper

Mike Horne

Robbie Kraike

Suzy Kraike

John Lovatt

Jayne Millington

Andrew Noble

Jack Noble

Richard Noble

Sally Noble

Adam Northcote-Wright

Steve O'Donnell

Brian Palmer

Leigh Remfry

Paul Remfry

Robin Richardson

Pete Ross

Ruth Stringer

Steve Wiltshire

Pegasus Microlight Team

Simon Blacker

John Fack

Richard Meredith-Hardy

Bill Sherlock

Mach 1 Club Platinum Members at Black Rock

Jim Cavanagh	Damien McCann
Jim Clark	Jason McCann
John Coppinger	Roger McCann
Matthew Cole	Barbie McSean
Rob Coy	Fred Patrick
Mike Dempsey	Allan Reid
Ian Denington	Doug Spence
Anthony Edwards	Robin Spence
Steve Francis	Brian Taylor
Duncan Garrett	Sarah Tilley
David George	Clive Tucker
Steve Georgii	Stanley Tucker
Damien Hawkins	Allan White
Bob Ibbertson	Andrew Whyte
Jonathan Lee	

UK Support Team

Nick Chapman

Neal Fletcher

Nigel Grant

Rob Hazell

SPEED
850 MPH
LIMIT